What would you do?

Richard Rozalewicz

BLUEROSE PUBLISHERS
India | U.K.

Copyright © Richard Rozalewicz 2023

All rights reserved by author. No part of this publication may be reproduced, stored in a retrieval system or transmitted in any form or by any means, electronic, mechanical, photocopying, recording or otherwise, without the prior permission of the author. Although every precaution has been taken to verify the accuracy of the information contained herein, the publisher assumes no responsibility for any errors or omissions. No liability is assumed for damages that may result from the use of information contained within.

BlueRose Publishers takes no responsibility for any damages, losses, or liabilities that may arise from the use or misuse of the information, products, or services provided in this publication.

For permissions requests or inquiries regarding this publication, please contact:

BLUEROSE PUBLISHERS
www.BlueRoseONE.com
info@bluerosepublishers.com
+91 8882 898 898
+4407342408967

ISBN: 978-93-5472-135-9

Cover design: Muskan Aggarwal
Typesetting: Rohit

First Edition: November 2023

This book is dedicated to:

My Sister, Michelle, is the toughest person I know and has had far more hurdles in life than I have. Battling from birth with learning difficulties and now the second time with cancer. She is the key reason I decided to write this book.

I'd also like to dedicate this book to some of my close family and friends, I will not share names but there are some that have had to endure terrible suffering from losing close loved ones through cancer.

To all those that are given their final ultimatum without being able to live out all their aspirations/purpose.

Acknowledgements

As already mentioned, my Sister Michelle was the inspiration for writing this book. Michelle, you have given me more motivation than you may ever know. Your tough, I will handle what life throws at me attitude is the epitome of being brave and strong. Your direct, no-filter stance is just perfect! Something I and others I am sure aspire to be more like at times. I can even imagine you seeing this book and thinking 'What a load of shit'. This puts a big smile on my face.

Thank you, Mum, for always being there for us, you have been such an incredible Mother, especially me, not being a very innocent child growing up. The amount of love and support you have given me, and Michelle has been unmeasurable.

Khaoula, for helping me get this book finished, you truly are a talented person, thank you so much!

Introduction

This is a self-help book. It is, albeit, slightly different to some of the other books in the same genre. What I can say for certain is that this book in particular transcends some of the more common motivational wisdom you expect to get from self-help-oriented content. The truth is, I am a very pragmatic, non-religious individual who's mostly focused on moving forward and making the most out of life. Why am I telling you this? Because it's important to me that you understand who you're listening to, and more importantly taking your precious time to read this book. I do not want to waste anyone's precious time. So, if after reading this introduction, you feel that it resonates with you on some level, or that it could guide you in some way to living a better life then, by all means, carry on.

I have to mention that while looking for inspiration for the book cover, I found a book titled "A Year to Live" by Stephen

Levine. It wasn't until this manuscript was finished that I made this discovery. How I missed this, I do not know! Be that as it may, I didn't want to publish this book without sharing that I was not aware that Stephen Levine's book existed until after writing this. Once I found out, I decided to read it. I have to say it's a very good book, and I thoroughly enjoyed reading it, but besides the common contextual concept of having one year to live, there are many differences in the content and approach that distinguish my work from Levine's. Either way, kudos to Stephen! Given that it is my first book and I did not realize the existence of a similar one -albeit only in title and general idea, I was not going to not publish it merely because of this reason. As I have already mentioned, my inspiration stemmed mainly from my dearest family members and friends being given their ultimatum, or prognosis in this sense.

Now, the reason I stated I am not religious is because it's pertinent and indicative of my thought process and decision-making ability. The whole concept of this book is based on only having one year to live, and using this notion to fuel your sense of direction and guide you on your path. Since religion is based on the belief that there exists something after death, this could limit how you choose to live your life (In my opinion). I am not against religion; I just do not believe in a god. This does not mean that this book can't help you if you are religious , it certainly can. I just want to be completely transparent about myself and what supports my thought process at times.

"It's a strange myth that atheists have nothing to live for. It's the opposite. We have nothing to die for. We have everything to live for."

— Ricky Gervais

This is a self-development book, and I know that tens of thousands of self-development books are published each year. So, how is mine any different you might ask? I have read many personal development books, and what I noticed is that besides some common patterns and topics (I have also included 4 chapters that cover common topics for the newbies in personal development, chapters 7-10), you tend to get consumed as a reader by new information and statistics without necessarily being prompted to act. This is one of the varying reasons why I wanted to write this book. I believe it to be just as pertinent for first-timers in self-development as it would be for more experienced individuals because it covers the basics, and it also offers a guide on moving forward in life using the 'one year to live' prognosis, along with the wheel of life to help guide where to focus your time. I don't claim to be an expert, and I don't think anybody can be completely in this field. It's a journey of continuous progress and development. I can, however, claim that I am fairly knowledgeable in this field given my many years of coaching and personal and professional history. This brings me to my other point; I don't want you to just read this book, I want you to use it as a guide. A kick-starter, if you will, that can help you firstly, discover what you want to do (if you don't know that already), and secondly, make a plan and figure out the steps you need to take to follow through with that plan. This is why this book exists. So, if you do decide to read it, then make sure to commit to the exercises and use the tools I have provided to get you from where you are to where you want to be, or at the very least, help you get started

I also want to share that most of what has been written in this book is not necessarily ground-breaking or unprecedented. Some of it you might have heard before, and some you might not be entirely familiar with. This book is rooted in the lifelong learnings I have picked up through research and experience. It's a compilation of concepts, ideas, values, and practices I believe to be correct, useful, and valuable - everyone is entitled to their personal opinion, right?

At this stage, I must confess that writing is not my primary profession. While I have dabbled in creating content for my podcast and the occasional article, the art of writing a book has proven to be a different beast altogether. I must admit that the journey has been filled with pauses and breaks (quite a substantial number, if I'm being honest). The inception of this project dates back to 2018, but it wasn't until later, in 2020, that I mustered the determination to see it through. Yet, even then, I took another hiatus until the end of 2022 before reigniting my efforts to complete this endeavor.

There is one particular aspect that deeply irks me, to put it mildly—it's when individuals fail to acknowledge the contributions of others and arrogantly claim sole credit for a collaborative effort. I have personally witnessed far too many instances where individuals shamelessly seize all the glory, disregarding the invaluable contributions of their peers. To those who engage in such behavior, I must say, shame on you!

With that in mind, I would like to say a big thank you to Khaoula for helping me get my thoughts down onto paper and supporting me with getting this book finished. Without your support, it could have easily taken me another two years!

And finally, what is this book about? Well, to be as concise as possible, it is about understanding if you are at a point where you want to make some changes in your life. It's about adopting the mindset of a person who only has one year to live and deciding where you want to go from there. This book will prompt you to think in unconventional ways and it will supplement that thinking with tools I have used in my professional and personal journey. Admittedly, some of these tools are not unheard of, but they are, in my humble opinion, tremendously helpful.

This is neither a complete nor comprehensive guide on how to live your life. There are some areas I discuss and examine which you can definitely find elsewhere. This is rather a catalyst to encourage you to act and, to provide you with structure and a strong sense of direction.

If you're looking for inspiration, you might be in the wrong place. I already stated that I am a practical individual, and that's what I believe this book is too, a practical guide on deciding where to move forward, and how to.

How to Read This Book

This book is split into two parts –

Part 1 is the one-year model/plan. Assessing where you are, dealing with your ego, wheel of life, bucket list, taking action, and finally, reflection.

Part 2 has four chapters designed for the common areas people tend to struggle with, which could be factors that stop you from achieving your one-year-to-live plan. Changing your state, focus, discipline and habit.

Throughout this book, you will find interactive activities designed to enhance your learning and personal growth. These activities are meant to help you actively apply the principles and strategies discussed. As I have already mentioned I encourage you to engage with these exercises to enrich your experience and understanding.

However, I understand that not everyone prefers to complete these activities within the book itself. That's why we've created a dedicated 'Resources' section on our website, richardrozalewicz.com, where you can find a wealth of information, downloads, and additional support for each of the activities presented in this book.

So, whether you prefer to work directly within these pages or opt for the digital resources available on our website, you'll find everything you need to make the most of this learning experience.

Contents

Part 1 One Year to Live
Chapter One: Do You Actually Want to Change?............2

Chapter Two Drop Your Ego 27

Chapter Three: What Would You Do If You Were Given One Year to Live? 51

Chapter four: What Is Your Plan? 82

Chapter Five: Time for Action...................................... 105

Chapter Six : Reflection and Measure 123

Part 2 Possible Roadblocks
Chapter Seven: How to Change Your State 138

Chapter Eight: How to Change Your Focus.................. 149

Chapter Nine: Discipline.. 162

Chapter Ten: Habits 171

Cheat Sheet.. 180

Part 1
One Year to Live

Chapter One:

Do you actually want to change?

We often move throughout our lives with very few moments of true contemplation (unless you are a serious meditator).. From the very beginning, we are instilled with ideas, ideas about how the world operates, ideas of good and evil, ideas of what we should be when we grow up, ideas of what path to follow, and what journeys are worth the hard work. Our parents taught us what their parents taught them and so on. This sounds like I am saying we have no free will, that everything we know and all we have become is a product of the environment we grew up in, the people we hung out with, or the outside influences that were introduced to us at some phase or another. That is the complete opposite of what I am trying to say in this book.

However, it's not an 'either /or' type of situation. Sometimes we operate on autopilot, we let all of our beliefs and the knowledge we accumulated about our surroundings guide our thoughts, feelings, behaviour, and decisions. Other times, we are more aware, more conscious, and more in the moment. It could happen when we're going through a life-altering event, something that makes us stop and rethink every step we've ever taken. More often, these contemplation moments occur when we, or our loved ones, face tragedy.

The Awful Truth

The truth is, we have always known the truth about life, about this world, and our collective fate as human beings. We, like the generations of people before us, are aware of our mortality, perhaps only at times. We know what death looks like from attending funerals, we know its palpable inevitability. We're constantly flooded with advice to make our lives worthwhile, to make the most out of this opportunity we've been given, to seek successes and accomplishments, to pursue happiness, and fulfilment, to live a meaningful life, to find our passion, our vocation, to mobilize all the tools at our disposal to leave a positive and indelible mark.

When we ponder over the fact that death is inevitable, we also face how unpredictable it can be. As a result, we're met with the pressure to do more, and be more. Suddenly we start questioning our entire existence, we think of all the time we've wasted on idleness, the relationships we've invested so much into that we've lost a part of ourselves in the process, and the fleeting thrills we've chased that brought us only bitterness and desolation. It comes as a surprise at first, almost like waking up after a bad dream, we're not sure of who we are nor where we stand.

And then the realization hits all at once, and we're fuelled by an irrepressible sense of motivation to uproot our lives and make loud and drastic changes (that can sometimes be a phase known as a 'midlife crisis'). We take the closest thing we have to an idol, someone we look up to, or a concept that fascinates us, and we try to embody their essence. We think that because we don't recognize the person we've become, we might as well reinvent ourselves into an ideal, no matter how intangible or unrealistic it might be. But like most projects we tend to undertake when we're blinded by the promise of a better us, this one too eventually fails or is left unfinished, hanging in the air like a threatening ghost, smoke from a pyre of burning hopes and dreams, withering away into the unknown.

This happens in cycles, first the dread and the depression, then a glimmer of hope, a blazing fire, inspiration, furious thoughts swarming in scraps and shreds, exhilaration, burnout, and back again, like a snake perpetually condemned to eat its own tail. It's morbid imagery, I admit, but I feel inclined to say it nonetheless because this book is not about pumping you up with false confidence or instilling you with deceitful and misleading assurances.

The Existential Overhaul

In order for us to get to the good, we, first, must go through the bad, navigate all the dilapidation, dot the i's, cross those t's, and dig deep to unearth all the thoughts, feelings, and beliefs we've internalized and suppressed, the very things that latched onto our minds like a parasite we cannot seem to detach our identities from, the things we think we are and the things we quiver before. The first step to take is this; putting everything out in the open, our darkest fears, and our deepest desires, they simply cannot remain unnamed, unknown, and unspecified. If we truly want to conquer the self-limitation within, we must first give it a name, a face, and an identity.

The confrontation needs to happen on a bright and cloudless day, where everything is what it seems to be, and where nothing disguises itself as what it isn't. Sometimes, we're not well-equipped to deal with or plan for grand schemes like finding meaning amidst the chaos, or preparing for our imminent demise so that on our deathbed, we're rather filled with felicity and joy of a life lived fully instead of regret and an unshakeable sense of failure.

When Tragedy Befalls

The longer you live, the more people you are likely to accompany to the threshold of death, to the point where you become familiar with the process, you know what comes next, but no matter how many partings you go through, you still don't feel confident to the extent that you would have absolutely no regrets if you were to draw your last breath in that very moment. Even those who have known of their terminal illnesses for months or years ahead often lament how unprepared they are to leave this plane of existence. In their final weeks, many people seek wisdom, reconciliation, healing, a second chance at personal growth.

It's almost a renaissance of some sort where people want to revive the spiritual part of their being and bring it forth to enjoy the small pleasures in life. Priorities shift and change, habits dissipate then reassemble, an empire falls down crashing, and a new one rises from the depths of its ashes. But why are we more profoundly open to experiencing the delights and tragedies of life only when we (or our loved ones) have been given a deadline, an expiration date?

Many people boast about catching themselves faltering and on the verge of plunging into a sunken rabbit hole just in the nick of time. They've seen the revival the consciously dying to get and they want to get a whiff of genuine fulfilment before it's 'too late.' Many of us have fallen victim to this thought. Yet kept delaying living our lives in accordance with our true values and authentic selves simply because it wasn't the 'right' moment, we had other more pressing matters to tend to, and our priorities resided with the people we were responsible for.

Compos Mentis

We've always seen taking care of our own needs and making sure they're being met on a daily basis as a selfish act, a rare indulgence. We pushed the lids on our hopes and dreams because there was always something more important to take care of, some more practical venture to follow. We learned that surviving in the real world meant there was no place for idealizations, fantasies, or fancy daydreams. We had to discipline our imagination, to suppress it, in eventual preparation for the ultimate sacrifice ritual, the muzzling ancient tradition of killing the delusional child to give birth to the lucid, sensible, and rational adult. Abolish lunacy, eradicate insanity, and ascend as compos mentis.

And so, all the infantile pleasures get pushed far down the well, they hide deep in the subconscious patiently waiting for the day to come when they are unleashed into the world. Because of this delay, some people begin to feel fragmented having left so many parts of their lives for 'later,' piles of unfinished business, and unfulfilled lifestyles. However, 'later' always comes sooner than we expect, sometimes much, much sooner when there is nothing left to mend.

Life is as perfidious as the waves, but it doesn't amount to the blind malevolence of time. Burdened by hollow dreams and a lugubrious sense of emptiness, we begin to experience the guilt and remorse of an unsatisfying work life, a neglected spiritual existence, and a futile attempt at cultivating our true hearts. If prompted to answer, most people will say that they would change everything about their lives if they knew they only had one year to live. They will craft the perfect bucket list, quit their job, go on adventures, explore the world, start a project, spend that quality time with family, study a language they've always wanted to learn, acquire a long-admired hobby, or skill, etc.

The more pessimistic kind will say 'if I have one year to live, I wouldn't change a thing, because what's the point really?' Perhaps it is pointless, but it is pointless regardless of whether we have one year or one hundred years to live. We are going to meet our downfall anyway, so I say why not go with a bang, why not make the most of our lives, why not strive

Stop Being a Passive Bystander

At times, it may feel like you're a passive participant in your life, an outsider, an onlooker, waiting for joy and success to come to you. You may even have neglected your inner self so many times that you don't know what you truly want anymore, you're not even sure if it's worth the time and effort to pursue anything at this point, you've become accustomed to the state you're currently in, comfortable in your own little bubble, refusing to let go of the knowledge you assembled in your own mind about the nature of the world. But you don't have to leave this world feeling like a failure, full of shame, fear, and regret because you were unable to navigate your life by the light of your authenticity, or because you couldn't honour your true self through your actions and behaviour.

You don't have to be a passive participant anymore, you don't have to sit and react to what the world throws at you, and you don't have to remain dissatisfied with yourself and the way you've lived your life so far. You can be an active participant, you can and should be the protagonist in your own journey, and you don't have to put your passions and interests aside because of your family responsibilities or societal norms. You are in control, you can buy that guitar you always wanted, that canvas stretcher you always dreamed of, and take that once-in-a-lifetime trip you always fantasized about.

You can awaken your dormant love of nature, take long meditative walks in the woods or sit by the sea and gaze at the crashing waves and mewing seagulls. You can push yourself out of your reading slump, and build that monumental library you have always visualized in your home. You can take up meditation, yoga, weight lifting, and running. You can change your dietary habits to a healthier and more balanced regimen. You can reconnect with old friends, nurture existing bonds, and cultivate new ones.

It's all about reclaiming your life, one step at a time. We tend to get impatient with ourselves, only allowing a certain number of chances, then anything beyond, we retract back to our shells with a crushing sense of defeat. But there is room, there is always room and that is what you should always keep in mind. There is room for improvement, there is room for change, not the windy and destructive type, but the exhilarating, uplifting, and exciting type.

You don't need to erase your identity and create a new one to live the life of your dreams. On the contrary, change is about the essentiality of healing and your willingness to invest in curative efforts. When faced with their terminal prognosis, many would say they'd have adopted a slower pace of life, minimized their attachment to material ambitions, changed their living space, or reduced their social circle to those whom they're closest to. Maybe they would have moved to a rural area, another country, another continent. Maybe they would have built the home of their dreams, or torn down a house inhabited by ominous ghosts from a painful, yet never distant past.

Though I am sure, most if not all of these people would do everything they can to get a few stolen moments where they get to appreciate the beauty of a wild rose bush, the distinct smell of earth before it rains, the enthralling melody of birds chirping in the morning, and the buzzing sound of bees pervading the crisp air of a delightful spring day. They would do their utmost to feel their titillating taste buds arouse upon taking a bite out of a decadent slice of chocolate cake, to draw a smile on the face of their loved one knowing they're the reason behind such elation, to envelop their arms around a long lost parent in a tight embrace, to feel the pleasure of their back floating and gently gliding in the serenity of the ocean with a breath-taking view of the soaring blue skies, the crisp salty air, the rippling blue water, and the warm rays of sunshine delicately seeping through a frosted billow of clouds.

Which Tense Are You Living In?

When we reminisce over our lives, we often notice our tendencies to take the picturesque for granted because we expect it to always be there, so we tell ourselves we will get to appreciate it when the time comes when we're not so pressed down by the millions of commitments and engagements we've made when we have room to breathe and be in the present moment. In the majority of cases, five years will go by, ten years even, decades, slipping away like water through cupped hands, and then we realize all that has been lost.

We think we missed our opportunity to make the change we've wanted and to rearrange our lives until they align with our core values. But this is what this book is about, and unless you're on your actual deathbed, then you still have a chance to redeem yourself so that you're proud of who you are, what you do, and how you do it. It may be too late to get into adrenaline-inducing hardcore or violent sports if you're suffering from the weariness that comes with old age, but other than agonizingly strenuous activity, you don't have to pull the plug on your dreams just yet!

You just have to want it, deeply, fervently, ardently, and more than anything you've ever imagined. We only get one chance at life, no take-backs, no redo's. So, for whichever reason you picked this book up, be it a desire to vanquish your fear of the unknown, cultivate the chance of dying consciously, or overcome your dread of an unconscious departure, the progression will be the same, that is to remember, to accept, to let go, and to trust the journey.

Get Over Your Fear of Life

The best and perhaps only approach to pierce through the impervious and get past the inaccessible is the life-affirming endeavour of mindfulness. This means learning the art of staying present, and in the moment, no matter how difficult the circumstances may be. Endurance is key and pushing through the spiritual, physical, and mental pains is a fundamental building block of insight, clarity, and closure. To learn the art of mindfulness requires that you first get over your fear of life.

We tend to think that death is the worst prognosis we can get, that in order for us to find true bliss, we need to look death in the face and scream at the top of our lungs "I'm not afraid of you!" But it is often our fear of life that prevents us from unleashing our fullest potential, accomplishing our goals, finding our purpose, and achieving our wildest dreams.

You've probably heard of fear of success, and while that phrase does sound like an oxymoron, something that isn't rational, that shouldn't even be uttered or thought of, it's that intense fear of success that makes us believe we are too be bludgeoned to accept our 'place' in the world.

We keep telling ourselves we're less deserving of success because there are smarter, better, more socially desirable people out there. That we got our piece of the pie, and no matter how meagre, we should be satisfied with those miserable slim pickings because there isn't enough for everyone out there. We make ourselves smaller and smaller, we think we're living with virtue when we accept our fate.

Anyone trying to change themselves or change the world must be naive, that their attempts at bettering their lives are destined to fail, and ultimately, they will know the bitter taste of disappointment and the reality of defeat. So, we live our whole lives on the surface, paddling around in a shallow pool of experiences, too afraid to take the plunge deep into the concentric well of wisdom and enlightenment. We're constantly caught up in the expansions of external stimuli, physical sensations, and furiously competing ideas that we rarely take a glimpse into the rippling delirium in waves of mutating tunes that our minds have created.

We're afraid of life, we're afraid of opening our hearts, we're afraid of reaching out, striking out, we're afraid of being ourselves, fully. We're convinced that these acts will put us in a vulnerable position and that we shouldn't pursue them because then we will get hurt, disappointed, angry, or frustrated. So, we keep building walls and fortresses to protect ourselves from the frightening possibility of overwhelming our egos, flooding our boundaries, and undermining our identities.

Every ounce of reason we possess disallows us to be more alive, and to experience the intensity of our emotions. We're perennially conflicted, on the one hand, we want to feel more, do more, and be more, but on the other hand, we find that very thought terrifying to the point where we constantly keep busy so as not to fall prey to our feelings, we keep running so we don't have to face ourselves, we numb ourselves to suppress our sense of being. And because we're so afraid of raw emotions, of the unrefined taste of life, we seek to control, power, and mastery over ourselves as well as over our surroundings.

We admire cool, calm, and collected people, those who don't show their emotions, those who calculate and anticipate, and those who never falter in their steps. We idolize unshakeable confidence, we revere discipline and, we worship restraint. Surely successful people got to where they are by sheer self-restraint and continence. Surely, they rose above their vulnerability and compulsion. Surely, they detached themselves from the feeble human shell to transcend as superior beings. The fundamental societal fealty to the core values of grandiloquence in achieving further reinforces these beliefs.

We're convinced that the modern individual's entire worth resides in how committed they are to being successful, more so than being a person. And thus, we all try to belong to this action-based and result-driven generation with an infallible motto to feel less and do more. So regardless of how we perform in our personal and professional lives, we will always be a failure as a person. This isn't meant to discourage you or minimize the successes you've achieved, on the contrary, it's meant to push you to acknowledge that sense of failure within yourself so you can overcome your fear of living.

We are often aware, on some level, of our pain, anguish, and despair, and we let our actions and behaviour drive us as we are determined to conquer our weaknesses and surmount our anxieties. This is why self-help and self-improvement books are so popular, but it's also why they fail to make us change permanently. Any feeling of motivation or inspiration fades as soon as we turn to the last page and close the book, then we begin to fall back into old habits, first disappointed, then angry that we allowed ourselves the chance to dream for a given moment, our thoughts a scrambled blur of guilt, shame, and confusion, "Did you truly believe this was it, your golden ticket to a new personality and a different life? How pitiable, how naive!"

The Art of Being

The truth is, being a person is not a performance to unlock, it's not something you practice. It requires that you cease your frantic business, that you take a step back to feel and breathe. When we do, we finally acknowledge how much pain we're in, the pain of not being ourselves, of not living up to our own standards, of not pursuing our true passion, and of not bothering to find our genuine purpose. Then there is an unmistakable comfort and glee in the thought that we may become whole, at long last. In the process of feeling our pain, we can finally develop the courage to accept it.

If we are willing to face our inner void, we will find fulfilment, and if we are willing to walk through our despair, we will find joy. So, are we, as modern beings, bound to a life of fear, a life of fearing life? Unfortunately, we are. We feel exhausted, drained, and depleted all the time because of this perpetual inner conflict. One part of ourselves is always in battle with the other part, always trying to overcome it, engulf it, swallow it whole to erase all trace of its existence. The ego is trying to control the physical body, the rational mind is trying to master the feelings, and the spirit is trying to override the fears, worries, and anxieties.

While this, in large part, occurs in our unconscious mind, its effects manifest on a more perceivable level, one which exhausts our energy and ravages our peace of mind. So, we try to run as far away as possible from these festering thoughts, we occupy ourselves, and we engage in monotonous conversations and brainless activities, all to avoid the monstrous clasp of our brains. But, we fail to recognize that tiny voice in our heads that keeps telling us, you are not enough, you will never succeed, you are destined to die without having accomplished a single endeavour to be proud of, your life will amount to nothing…

Beware of self-fulfilling prophecies

We seldom perceive negative self-talk as what it is. Often, we take these words, internalize them, and repeat them to ourselves like an oracle does a prophecy. Negative things that we've been told hold a far greater power as we use them to dig our own graves, to fashion a cloak we conceal ourselves within, wearing it disgracefully like a badge of dishonour. And because of the things we've been told, the things we tell ourselves, we start to lose faith in our ability to change. Our pessimistic deliberation was suspended like a curse, a self-fulfilling prophecy. It sounds almost prosaic, the idea that we are the architects of our own destruction. It's a very Greek idea, and a profound one too.

We believe we are incapable of change because we've already been made to fulfil a given role, and besides that one designation, there is no other part, duty, or function we can execute. Some people believe that in order to deliver themselves from the curse, they need to repress all the feelings and memories they associate with their fears. But repression does not stop your fears from unfolding, on the contrary, it binds you to those fears as you are programmed to fall into them later in life. We can understand this better through Greek tragedies, most notably the story of Oedipus.

Laius abandoned his son after learning from the oracle of Delphi that Oedipus will kill him one day and marry his mother (Laius's wife). But, Oedipus doesn't die like Laius intended him to. Instead, he is raised by the king and queen of Corinth. Once he grew up, he learned about the prophecy from the same source and fled Corinth for Thebes (where his biological parents reside) to avert the prophecy, not knowing that the people who raised him were not his real parents. Upon his arrival, Oedipus ends up killing Laius (whom he doesn't know to be his father) in a quarrel.

Do you actually want to change?

Then after defeating the sphinx, he wins the throne of Thebes and marries his own mother. Self-fulfilling prophecies often manifest as unconscious behaviour, where our predictions about ourselves and who we think we are often come true, not because they're indubitably correct, but because we believe in them so ardently that all of our instincts and actions bring that reality to pass. There are countless examples of self-fulfilling prophecies in classic literature, one particularly striking, "Appointment in Samarra" by John O'Hara. This novel perfectly illustrates the self-destruction of its main character, Julian English.

The epigraph of this book is perhaps most telling and relates directly to the title, probably the author's take at painting a picture to foreshadow the events of his story. This, in fact, is a popular ancient Mesopotamian tale about a merchant in Baghdad who sends his servant to the marketplace to acquire some provisions. Soon afterwards, the servant comes back shaken and frantic, and he tells his master how he was jostled by a woman in the market whom he recognized to be Death. He recalls the events saying that the woman threatened him and begs the merchant to borrow a horse so he can flee to Samarra, a city 125 km away, where he believes Death won't be able to find him.

The merchant then goes to the marketplace to find Death. Once he gets to the woman he asks her why she threatened his servant. Death says she didn't threaten the merchant, that her arm went up in surprise simply because she was not expecting the servant to be in Baghdad, "you see I have an appointment with him tonight in Samarra." O'Hara describes the title he chose as a reference to the inevitability of Julian English's death.

All of these stories serve to tell us that our attempts at escaping 'fate' only serve to make that fate more imminent and binding. What we fail to acknowledge is how decisive of a part we play, an active one, if unconscious, to create that fate. And so, the defences we put up that are meant to protect us from fulfilling those dreaded prophecies end up producing the very conditions and circumstances we aim to avoid. But, when we build walls around us to protect ourselves, don't we become prisoners in our fortresses? It is as hard for us to get out of that entrapment as it is for others to penetrate it.

Whether it be a fear of rejection, a fear of failure, a fear of weakness, etc, when we try to overcome those 'personality issues' by denying them, we further internalize the issue and thus ensure its continuance. And yet we keep trying to override our guilts, fears, anxieties, and weaknesses because we believe that surmounting inner obstacles is the only way to fulfil our dreams and overcome what has been holding us back for decades. Our willpower is effective in performing and achieving, but it is also completely obsolete when it comes to altering the inner state of our existence. Our feelings and emotions are not subject to our willpower. Suppressing them doesn't make them go away, it only pushes them deep down where they cannot be seen by the naked eye.

There are fundamental ways in which we create our own fate (or design our own destruction per se). First, through our attitude and behaviour, so based on our distinctive characteristics, we invite certain reactions and responses from those around us that reinforce our perception of ourselves. And second, by acting upon our fears within ourselves so that we perpetrate the fate we seek to evade perpetually. Because we project these facts we know about ourselves and this knowledge we've accumulated over the years into the world, we unconsciously make the outer circumstances match the inner situation.

Where Exactly Are You in Your Life Right Now?

If you actually want to change, you can't expect to overcome an issue that is part of your personality, because in doing that you're turning one part of yourself, the ego, against the other, the willpower. So instead of a harmonious coexistence between these two contrasting entities of human nature, you're creating conflict, an insolvency that will ultimately destroy you as a person. The healthier alternative can only happen through kindness, compassion, and understanding, which will eventually lead to self-acceptance.

When we begin to understand the correspondence between our inner condition and external factors, we learn more about human nature than any other insightful tool can claim to offer. We tend to get extremely uncomfortable when we find ourselves in alien situations, situations that we're not familiar with, that we've never encountered before. And most people's first instinct is to choose flight over fight. As human beings, we are creatures of habit, our bodies, minds, and behaviour become conditioned by a variety of elements and situations, which makes it incredibly difficult for us to adapt and adjust to different circumstances. Regardless of the state we're born in, what truly determines who we are, what seals our fate, and determines our destiny is how we are raised. So, to encounter true change, change that transcends the ego and the willpower, change that lasts, is the most meaningful journey you can embark on in this life, but also the most difficult.

So, do you actually want to change? What phase in life are you currently in? What is this phase teaching you? What are you holding on to that is limiting you? Do you want to create more room just to be? Are you accepting of the changes in your life? What mindset are you pursuing? Are your thoughts your own? Are they someone else's? Can you tell what beliefs are attached to those thoughts? Did that belief serve its purpose? Can you let it go now? Can you be thankful for the challenges you've encountered? Is there anything you're taking for granted that you should be grateful for? What are you afraid of? What do you fear in life that may bring you unimaginable pain? What is your purpose in life? Is this the direction you want to be moving in? Are your recent choices helping you? What has to happen so that you are finally able to make the changes you want to see in your life? If you don't change, where will you be in a year's time? What will you miss out on? ... If not now, when?

So, what matters the most to you?

This is one of the many questions I will ask you to consider and reconsider profoundly throughout this book -and perhaps for the rest of your life. Most people don't give it much thought until it's too late and they're on their deathbed. I don't want

Do you actually want to change?

that to happen to you, I don't want you to realize your life's true purpose only when you're unable to act upon it.

To conclude this chapter, I am going to walk you through two exercises that will allow you to connect with what you want from this life. These exercises will involve you thinking about your own death, in detail. Although frightening, they are very powerful tools that can provide you with the clarity you need so you can begin working on what you want your life to stand for.

We've already established the inevitability of death. Yes, sometimes it can be delayed, but it can't be avoided. You can't control how you die or when, but you can control how you choose to approach life from this day forward. When you have a close encounter with death, even a subtle brush, your life changes in a dramatic way. Getting that close to the end forces most individuals to take stock and reconsider what they've been doing this entire time.

When the veil separating life and death is lifted, something clicks, and people realize the only viable option is to wake up and start pursuing the things that are meaningful and worthwhile to them. They know they have to spend the remainder of their days doing things that matter to them, things that will leave a positive impact, it's their legacy after all. The following exercise will help you connect with the things you want to be remembered for.

Exercise: Death Meditation

It's your funeral. Everything is set. The casket, the chief mourners, the family bearers, the car, the guests, the flower arrangements... Visualize the scene as if you were there. You can see yourself in the open casket, you can hear the faint music. Take a closer look. Who are the attendees? You spot your family, friends, and loved ones, perhaps some of your neighbours, colleagues and former classmates from way back.

Now, listen to the things they're saying about you. Listen to the words coming out of their mouths, the comments you wholeheartedly want them to make, the things you want to hear them say about you. Take a deep breath and don't leave the scene. Simply lean back, keep your eyes closed, and focus on what you've heard (from your partner, kids, best friends, colleagues…). Now take a moment and write everything down.

What people said about me

_____
_____
_____
_____
_____

What I wanted people to say about me

_____
_____
_____
_____
_____

Do you actually want to change?

The takeaway from this exercise is that each thing you 'heard' and wrote down reflects a deeper part of who you are, what core values you hold in high regard, and what you would like your life to be about. What you heard other people say about you, reflects your lifestyle. Perhaps some comments may have been disappointing or they may have filled you with regret. Maybe one of the people said "he had so much potential that he left unfulfilled", or "if only he could overcome his fears, I wonder what tremendous things he would have been able to accomplish." Fortunately, you're not dead yet, which means you still have time to overturn the verdict and start living in a way you want to be remembered. The reason why you need to do this exercise is also practical in a way that allows you to gain perspective into your inner workings and understand your life through the actions you took.

This next exercise builds upon the findings of the first one and will help you determine what you truly care about in life if you weren't inhibited by the things holding you back. This is definitely a scary one too (especially if you're not very fond of visualizing your own death, but then again, this is the whole premise of this book). But, if you choose to go through with it, even if it upsets or unsettles you, you will connect with what matters to you in life. So again, take your time, find a quiet space for honest and open reflection, sit, and contemplate.

Exercise: Epitaph Writing

Part A

For this exercise, you will need to write your own epitaph. This is the inscription of your gravestone as it would be designed if you were to die today. What would your epitaph say if you left this plane of existence without fulfilling your goals, dreams, and passions? What would the text be if you didn't live with purpose if you didn't lead a life that aligns with your core values and principles?

Be mindful of all the things you wanted to do that were left unfinished simply because you were too scared to see them through. Think of all the projects you've thought about starting that you never did because you allowed your doubts and worries to get in the way. Think of the self-limiting beliefs, the negative self-talk, the self-deprecation ... List all the reasons that kept you from unleashing your full potential. Then write it all down!

Here Lies

_____

_____

_____

_____

_____

This was difficult, wasn't it?

This exercise forced you to face some of your deepest fears, perhaps even a few catalysts of shame, guilt, and embarrassment. However, it was necessary. You can't make lasting changes if you don't look death in the face and fight your way back to life.

Part B

The second part of this exercise will be much more inspiring. I'd like you to rewrite your epitaph, only this time, you write it as if you fulfilled your dreams and aspirations. Write an epitaph you will be proud of, one that paints a positive picture of yourself, one that summarizes all the great things you've accomplished. Think of this epitaph as a direct representation of all the things that matter to you the most, the things you truly care about, and the things you wish to be renowned for.

Imagine you could live the life of your dreams. No fear, no doubt, no worries. What would you do on a typical day? What would you like to stand for? As you consider these questions, visualize your headstone. What words are inscribed there? What is written in your epitaph? Think of a series of statements that best encapsulate the essence of your dream life. What do you want to be remembered for? If you could live a life free of fear, what would you invest your time and energy in?

Here Lies

_____

_____

_____

_____

_____

This exercise isn't merely hypothetical. You are basically planning for your true epitaph, so what you will be known for and what defines your life are entirely up to you. It's all based on the actions you choose to take right this moment. This is how you determine what people say about you at your funeral, and this is how you (although metaphorically) write your own epitaph.

When you're done, compare the script from Part A with the script from Part B. Place them side by side and spot the differences. Not every goal you accomplish will be there, but the things that are most important to you, the things you've worked for, the values you held and lived by, will be. If you're not living a life that is true to your values, then you're not the person you want to be. Now is the time to make changes and now is the time to live the life you want and do the things that matter to you!

Chapter Two

Drop Your Ego

We all had childhood dreams of whom we wanted to be when we grew up, visions of what we wanted our lives to look like. We've felt a grand sense of purpose as if we were destined to do great things. We had a clear idea of the persona we wanted to embody, and we believed in our abilities to make it come true. Perhaps you wanted to be an Athlete, Rockstar, an Astronaut, or something else entirely. You knew, with absolute certainty, who you were and what you wanted out of life. You were also confident in your ability to turn those dreams into your reality. Often, you would fantasize about the future and the life your future self would be leading. You see yourself as the hero, the protagonist in your own story. Fast forward to today and you may not be leading the life you envisioned for yourself.

One year to live

The truth is, as we grow up, we're forced to let go of some of our thoughts, ideas, and dreams. We soon come to learn that the 'real world' does not tolerate daydreaming or idealism. We're told we have to snap back to reality if we want to make it in this modern day and age. To more seasoned outsiders, our hopeful dreams and optimistic goals seem to be verging on the delusional. They tell us that failure is inevitable, that our vision for our own future is absurd and impossible to achieve. We're too naive, too idealistic, too eager, too gullible ...

So, we keep taking on those NOs, we internalize that rejection, pessimism, and hopelessness as our own. We absorb the conventional norms of what realism means, and what surviving in the real-world entails. Each dark and sceptic interjection suppresses our childhood dreams deeper and deeper into our minds and after a few years (or decades), we're all grown and those dreams are long gone. We never fully realize it, of course, unless you're thrown into a 'one year to live' type of scenario. Bitterness has the tendency to creep up on you.

When we're younger, we care too much, we give too much, and we love too much. We're still not entirely aware of the crushing aftermath of fear, sadness, tragedy, and disappointment. We haven't been hurt to the point of no return yet. We still have expectations of life, ourselves, and others. We're confident in our ability to bounce back when the going gets tough. There is a cumulative effect of being betrayed, let down, hurt, and disappointed. Then those negative experiences begin to snowball and all we're left with is bitterness, misery, and desolation.

As kids or teenagers, we were impatient to move into adulthood. We looked forward to being free, independent, and making our own decisions. But the more autonomy we gain, the less satisfied we are with the state of our lives. We have some of the tools and some of the knowledge, we have the freedom and the ability, so why aren't we living the life we envisioned for ourselves? What happened between now and then that put us in this doleful position? How many times have you found yourself fantasizing about the life of your dreams, only for your inner critic to stomp on those thoughts with utter disdain, "as if that's ever going to happen to you…?"

It's safe to say that everyone's been guilty of this at one point or another. You take that criticism to heart and you scold yourself for even entertaining such fanciful ideas. You know exactly how dwelling on your own imaginings ends up. It only makes you sad, and disappointed, or angry and disappointed, neither is a good combination. You're convinced it won't lead you anywhere, if anything, it will derail you from more practical and more pressing issues.

Meet your ego

We all want to create a comfortable environment for ourselves, our families, and our loved ones. We're told that if we abide by the rules and if we go with the flow then life will be stable, peaceful, and fulfilling. And that works, to a certain extent, and with certain people. For many, these are the wrong ingredients for a satisfying life. You followed societal norms, you've set your ambitions aside, you landed a job in a lucrative field, your career picked up, and you found yourself mastering the strange role of a corporate professional. You're driven, and focused, you're rising through the ranks at an impressive pace.

Your days are packed with commitments and engagement that your inner self does not care much for. You fill your house with things you don't need and fill your time with people you don't enjoy being around. The cacophony suffocates your inner thoughts and for a while, it's fun. You feel like you're living a life that isn't yours. But the freaky Friday effect soon wears off and depression creeps in.

In your rush to progress, get ahead, and achieve other people's idea of success, you realize that all this time you were compensating for something that was missing from your life, something you didn't even realize you lost. If you're lucky, you get that ephemeral yet compelling moment of clarity when you realize you've been chasing after society's definition of success. We'd like to believe that at that moment, we'll be filled with a sense of serenity and harmony, having unlocked one of the precious secrets the universe is so reluctant to bequeath, at least to the 'unworthy.'

Unfortunately, that moment often feels like a violent punch in the face, you're sick to your stomach, you're filled with dread, and you're anxious over all the years you've wasted not chasing your higher purpose. Like so many others, we tend to value success over purpose, and recognition over authenticity.

What would we do if there was no one left to impress, what then? Where are these thoughts coming from? Why are you feeling contemptuous? Why are you feeling insecure? Why do you care so much about how others see you? The thoughts and suspended questions are taunting you, and you try to come up with answers.

Because I feel embarrassed, because I'm afraid to give up a comfortable and stable life for a dream, a promise because I don't want to be a failure, because I need other people's approval and validation to compensate for my insecurities, because I'm afraid I'm lacking something that other people possess, because I'm scared I won't find happiness in what I want, because I want others to see me as practical and rational, I want to exude confidence, not look like someone who's driven by their emotions and feelings.

Bingo! You've just discovered your ego.

The realization alone will not save you from your ego. It will fight back, and your thoughts will pull and push. Your ego will refuse to relinquish the control and power it has. Often, you will come to believe that you and your ego are one, an inseparable entity, but it's important that you know you are not!

The EGO is the 'what' and the 'why.' The ego is what prevents us from following our dreams because it tells us we should take the path others expect us to, and make decisions that align with the norms and ideals of the people around us. What is and isn't acceptable to our social group becomes the key focus whenever we begin a new venture. God forbid we offend our peers with too avant-garde ideas of success and happiness. So instead of focusing on our own happiness, instead of working on accomplishing our wildest goals, we're too afraid to stand out, too anxious to come across as different or unconventional because, in our minds, that will only lead to isolation and ridicule. So, we grieve our losses and decide to settle for what is convenient, conventional, socially acceptable, and -often- awfully dull.

What is ego?

You might be wondering why the ego has such a strong grip on who we are, what we do, and how we choose to live our lives. You might even be wondering what the ego is in the first place. This word is thrown around all the time that it somewhat lost its original meaning. We tend to associate the ego with being arrogant, selfish, and full of oneself. Yet, we fail to realize that the ego isn't the consequence, it's rather the cause. According to Sigmund Freud, we human beings are very complex, and our personalities consist of more than a single component. Freud defines this in three main elements: the id, the ego, and the superego.

These three elements tend to work together but they each have their unique function. The interaction of the three components has a powerful influence on human thought and behaviour. These elements also emerge at different points in our lives. The id, for instance, is present since birth and represents more primitive and instinctive behaviour. It is driven by a compelling sense of hedonism as its main goal is to seek pleasure and instant gratification of all wants and needs. If these desires and needs go unmet, this results in a state of anxiety and tension.

The id is a vital component of personality because it ensures the infant's needs are met. People eventually learn to control this part of themselves through the emergence and development of the ego and superego but the id's primal force is always there. The ego, on the other hand, is developed to manifest the id's wants and needs in a way that is acceptable to the outside world. This element is responsible for dealing with reality, hence striving to fulfil the id's desires in appropriate and realistic ways.

This principle pushes people to weigh the risks and benefits of an action before they make the decision to pursue or abandon their impulses. More often than not, the id's demands can be satisfied but only at a certain time and place, this process is known as delayed gratification. The ego helps discharge tension built up as a result of unfulfilled impulses by seeking something in the real world that resembles the mental image the id created, this is called secondary process thinking.

The superego is all about moral standards and ideals that we acquire from our surrounding environment. This includes our idea of what right and wrong are as well as what makes sound and unbiased judgments. So, the ego's sole job is to ensure we get what we want (in realistic ways) while protecting us from being harmed, both physically and emotionally. This thought process means the ego only cares about itself, so all attempts made by it are for sheer self-preservation. The ego believes that it exists separately, detached from other entities. This is where the 'us versus them' mindset comes from. It wants to keep the id happy (within societal standards), but the ego's perception of the world is false and inaccurate. It takes everything personally and strives to be in control at all times. It's the part within us that is always self-conscious, constantly comparing and complaining, and often acting as a fear-mongering agent.

Fear is your ego's attempt to prevent you from getting into a situation that is completely unfamiliar to you. When this happens, the ego wants to be in the driver's seat. It takes charge of the situation by creating different levels of fear to maintain control, keep you feeling small, and stop you from venturing outside of your comfort zone. The ego feels responsible for your safety, personal interests, reputation, and survival. It seeks to separate you from your surroundings, which can leave you feeling out of tune and full of distress. Because of these properties, your ego will often prevent you from not just achieving your dreams, but dismissing them before they're formed into thought in the first place.

You are not your ego.

Your ego is the voice of dissatisfaction in your mind. It could go by, undetected for years, but it's always there, it's always been there. You never notice your ego because you assume that it's the real you. But you are not your ego and you are not your thoughts. You are your consciousness, that which lies beneath all the mental activity. Like rippling waves on the shore, the mind is unpredictable, it always tries to swirl with the tide, but your truest form is that which lies beneath the ripples. Your ego speaks from a mindset of scarcity, not one of abundance.

I need to be successful; I need to get attention; I need other people to approve of who I am and validate what I do.

These are false narratives that your ego creates to justify and compensate for that scarcity. The reality you live in often stems from the stories you tell yourself. This is how powerful your thoughts are, and how dominant your self-talk is.

When you realize this, you know that in order for you to transform your life, you need to change the story you tell yourself. Most importantly, you need to find one that transcends your ego. Your ego tells you to worry about the future, to lament the past, to stay fixated on the mistakes you made, to constantly doubt yourself, it makes you believe you're the victim of circumstance. It's everywhere all at once, except where it matters the most, the present moment.

Every beginning necessitates an end.

Knowing how strong of a grasp your ego has on your mind is not enough. In order for you to truly free yourself from the shackles that have been holding you back all these years, you need to be prepared to let go of limiting beliefs to free up room for your true self to shine. Like a snake, you must shed that old layer of skin so a new one, an improved one, can take its place. In a physical sense, we do this on a daily basis.

The average person generates about seventy billion cells per day to replace dead ones. After seven years, every cell in their body has died and been replaced. Matter keeps changing from one state to the other. It's alive and it's constantly moving. And so, we're destined to follow this inescapable choreography, a dance of life where first we crawl, then we walk, we run, we fly, we crash, we rise, and we're right back where we started.

We reflect on that journey and how it impacted us then we prepare ourselves for the next one. In order for us to continue to grow, the obsolete parts of ourselves, the ones we no longer have use for, the ones that are only holding us back, and keeping us chained must die. Just like shedding dead cells is essential to the proper functioning of our bodies, shedding old ideas and beliefs that don't serve us anymore is essential to the growth of our consciousness. And, so in this chapter, you will learn how to shed the ferocious layers of the ego, one limiting belief at a time.

Welcome to the real world, it's all downhill from here.

Long ago, before you developed the strikingly masochistic ability for doubt, judgment, and insecurity, your ego did not exist. You couldn't yet tell the difference between who you were and the vast consciousness that you came from. In a way, you were and felt complete. Now, your ego says "Look at you, look at your bank account, look at your life, one mistake after the other, one bad decision after the other, you're a failure." I hate to break it to you but you have no higher purpose, it's this or nothing, you're doomed, you will always be miserable, you will never amount to anything, and there is no 'bright' future to look forward to. Welcome to the real world! It's all downhill from here."

Your mind is spinning. Is it true? Have you been foolish to believe that you could actually change your life in one year? That you could become the person you always wanted to be, that you would find happiness and fulfilment, that you would finally discover your purpose and conquer your fears, all in what, a year? What does your ego say to this? I doubt; therefore, I think, I think, therefore, I am ... everything.

But, you are not your thoughts. Just because your ego mind says something, it does not make it true. You're not your ego-mind, you're not the doubt and fears and anxieties. You're not the depression, you're not the limiting beliefs, you're not a victim of your surroundings, of circumstances, of society, nor of the world. You're the pool of consciousness from which those thoughts arise. Don't identify with the ripples. Don't let them take over. Detach yourself of your ego, of its perversities and caprices, of its violent mood swings and irrational fits. Only when you do so will you be able to identify which thoughts should be ignored and discarded and which thoughts should be developed and nurtured?

You've learned about the Freudian ego, that, unlike the id's passions and fixations, it represents logic, reason, and sanity. It's your mind's police, and it's what keeps your animal instincts in check so that you can operate within the confines of an organized society. What Freud failed to mention, however, is that the ego is proud, judgmental, manipulative, and often self-deprecating.

While he was right about the function of the ego in managing your irrational behaviour, he didn't acknowledge the ego's tendency to hijack your consciousness, and in its attempt to suppress the lower self, it also suppresses the higher self. It cannot fully grasp the difference between the two.

Your ego sees the world from its own -often very limited perspective, and so its understanding of the world is deeply rooted in that limitation. In this context, the ego can be a useful assistant, but it simply shouldn't be left alone in the control room.

Free your mind

Society is built on shared values, common understandings of right and wrong, and mutually held agreements. For instance, we have agreed to make money as an instrument for exchange. We made an agreement to wear clothes outside, to respect each other's property and personal space, and we even agreed to give up some of our freedom for security. Most of the clauses in this social agreement are reasonable and logical. They just make sense and intend to make our lives more structured, organized, and stable.

With that said some agreements society has issued can be more counterproductive than useful. For example, there is an unspoken standard that only people who come from an elite social class and attend prestigious schools can know true success. While many enjoy rooting for the underdog, very few expect them to actually make it to the big leagues, while most settle for a somewhat favourable outcome.

Moreover, society tells us that if you voice an unpopular opinion, then you will be faced with rejection, disdain, and even ridicule. If you challenge how things stand, you will fail. If you pursue happiness, you're delusional. If you chase wealth, you're materialistic. If you want to find love, you're hopeless. If you're too picky, if you have high standards, if you don't want to settle, you're a fool and an idealist.

The worst thing about these 'agreements' and limitations, is that the people who are constantly reminding you of what ought to be, do so because they think they're serving your best interests when in reality they're doing the very opposite. The social contract serves to limit your potential and tame the burning fire inside you. You can't be unpredictable, you can't be erratic, impulsive, passionate, spontaneous.

You have to fit the standard, you have to be stripped of the power that can potentially push you to disturb the status quo. It's not some big conspiracy that everybody else is in on, it's just how things are. Or so your ego wants you to believe. And so, what happens when you find yourself pushing against some of the counterproductive social agreements? Your ego tells you it's no use to resist, it wants you to avoid the problem, abandon the situation, and quit while you're still ahead. But often, when you avoid the problem, you also avoid the solution.

Change your focus, change your life.

Picture this; you walk into somebody else's house, somewhere you've never been before, you look around, what jumps to you first? Is it the picture frames, the torn wallpaper, how the sofas are arranged, the scattered toys, or is it the smell coming from the kitchen, the cold velvety feel when you touch the dusty curtains, the shuffling sound as you drag your feet across the carpet? Now, what if another person were to walk into that same house, would they take notice of all the things you did? Would they be interested in the details that sparked your curiosity? The setting is the same but their attention would be drawn to different things. What if ten other people entered the same house? Then you will get ten different experiences and interpretations of that space.

This doesn't mean they are not accurate, on the contrary, they all are but they just don't represent the whole truth, they are fragments of the truth. In the same way, people perceive reality through their own perspective, which means the experiences they have are personal and subjective.

Everything that occurs in that reality is up for interpretation based on who you are, what you value, how you see the world, and so on. Your reality is filtered through what you perceive much like it is for others and what they perceive. So, what makes the distinction between your reality and that of other people around you? The answer is your focus.

When you change your focus, you can change your perception, your reality, and by extension your life. For instance, when you fixate on how stressful your job is, your focus generates more stress. When you focus on how anxious or nervous you are in a social setting, your attention causes those feelings to amplify because it's all you can think of at that given moment.

In that way, whatever you put your focus on becomes your perceived reality. So, when you worry about all the problems you have and how impossible they seem, you're directing your mind towards all the negative repercussion that problem has on your life, this puts your focus on the obstacle itself and what it entails, but not the solution. However, when you shift your focus, your subjective reality also takes a turn, and your circumstances do too as they move to represent that shift in perspective.

How to drop your toxic ego?

Before moving forward with a plan on how to conquer your one year to live, you need to drop your toxic ego first. You can't have it in the way because it's one of the biggest roadblocks, if not the biggest. The truth is, most people with a stopwatch in their life will feel inclined to drop their ego and allow themselves to pursue their purpose and do what makes them truly happy without fear of others and without any hesitation. They are already aware of what's at stake here and they know they won't get a second chance.

Detaching yourself from your ego will allow you to move freely in your thoughts and aspirations and to finally be happy with no burden of being scared of what other people might think or say. Now freeing yourself from the clutches of your ego sounds thrilling. You're driven by the promise that your life will change for the better once your ego is out of the way, but sometimes, this process can be difficult. This is a part of yourself that you have to relinquish, or at the very least, take more control over. It's certainly a challenge, however, with the right amount of focus and determination, this shift becomes more achievable.

Below is a list of exercises that will teach you how you can let go of your toxic ego. Make sure to implement these before you move forward with this book, otherwise, the upcoming chapters won't make much of an impact if you're still holding onto those limiting beliefs.

1. Adopt a beginner's mindset

Epictetus says "It is impossible to learn that which one thinks one already knows." You can't learn if you're convinced you already know everything that is worth knowing. You can't improve if you already think you are the best. And you won't be able to find the answers if you're too conceited to know how to ask the questions in the first place. When you allow your ego to believe that it already knows everything, it convinces itself of its own genius, perfection, and innovation, which makes it much harder to accept feedback that does not align with its own assessment of itself.

If you truly want to drop your ego, you need to adopt a beginner's mindset and be willing to open yourself up to a new world of knowledge. To become the person, you ultimately hope to become, humility is essential because it's what tells you that you don't know enough, and therefore need to keep studying. The ego likes to jump to the end telling you that patience is a weakness, that it's for losers, and that you're ready to share your talents with the world.

2. Focus on effort instead of expectations

Marcus Aurelius said, "Ambition means tying your well-being to what other people say or do. Sanity means tying it to your own actions." Your one-year to live plan will not always go smoothly. You will fail, and you will feel sabotaged, unappreciated, frustrated, and even angry. You will come across obstacles that may seem insurmountable. Your ego will make you question everything. It will try to derail you from the path ahead. It will want to take over and put you back in your previous state. It will want to restore what it knows to be 'order.' It will resist more than you would think.

How do you carry on then? How do you remind yourself of what matters? How do you find encouragement when everything seems to be going to hell? You focus on effort rather than expectations. Coach John Wooden defines success as " Peace of mind, which is a direct result of self-satisfaction in knowing you made the effort to do your best to become the best that you are capable of becoming."

3. Choose purpose, not passion

Many people sink their own ships before they even get a chance to leave the harbour. Like every other uninitiated, they had the burning passion, the eagerness, the zeal, the enthusiasm, even the willingness to tackle everything at hand, yet they lacked something crucial, something that the bundle of energy they have cannot make up for, and that is the purpose.

When your purpose is much bigger than who you are, then everything becomes much easier in the sense that you now know what it is you need to do and what matters the most to you. When that occurs, you can begin to let go of other thoughts that you're able to discern as mere distractions. But, just to be clear, passion is also critical. Passion is about emotions, motivation and what makes us feel good, i.e. "do what you love". The purpose is the reason or the why behind what we do, primarily for others, i.e., "do what contributes." Where passion can be all over the place, wild and exciting, purpose is much more focused.

4. Ignore the talk and do the work

Talking and doing often require the same resources and the same energy. The fact is, talk tends to make you feel depleted and research suggests that at some point your mind will start to confuse goal visualization for actual progress. The same goes for verbalizing that visualization. When you spend a lot of time thinking about a given task or a goal, explaining it to yourself, and talking about it, you feel much closer to the outcome despite not having done anything yet.

What is dangerous about this is that when you try to accomplish that goal and it turns out to be more challenging than you thought, you could put it aside or let it go simply because you believe that you've done your best and any further attempts will just be fruitless. That's how harmful talk can be. So instead of depleting your resources to fuel that talk, shut up, stay accountable, and focus on doing the work.

5. Kill your pride

Many religions consider pride to be a sin because it's a false narrative people tend to feed themselves. Pride can convince you that you're so much better than you actually are, even better than God or some other higher power. Pride feeds arrogance and leads people away from humility. With that said, you don't need to be religious to find wisdom in this idea. You need only to care about your personal growth and development to understand that pride can be a dangerous distraction and a threatening deceiver.

Your ability to learn, acquire new skills, implement action, to adapt, to build resiliency, and to establish connections with others can be dampened by your pride. Pride can take a small achievement and blow it out of proportion to make it seem like a huge one. There's no harm in celebrating small victories, but you mustn't lose focus on how much work is left to be done, otherwise, you will fall prey to inaction and stagnation.

6. Stop romanticizing the grand narrative

When you're aspiring to achieve a number of goals, you have to resist the urge to reverse engineer the success of other people's narratives. And when you do achieve the levels of success you aspired to, you have to resist the impulse to pretend that everything unfolded exactly how you intended it to, despite how great that makes you sound or how much of a boost it gives to your self-esteem.

There is no grand narrative and you can attest to that because you will be there watching your journey unravel. Developing a conviction that you're going to change the world or revolutionize a given industry is not bad, but those ideals can easily get you to a stuck point where you're too paralyzed by the perfectionist concepts you have that you can't get yourself to execute them or bring them into reality.

You can have disruptive and frighteningly ambitious goals but you have to accept that your starting point will consist of a small one. You simply don't start with a violent frontal attack, you have to initiate the process with a modest bet and continuously build your ambitions as you go. Focus on the work and the values behind your ambitions, not some grand or glorious vision that sounds good or read well in writing.

7. Learn to better manage yourself

Managing yourself is much harder than if somebody else were to manage you, it requires a special level of dedication, determination, and discipline. Some people are driven by the feedback they receive from others, the deadlines they're allocated, the kind of progress tracking that keeps them accountable, and so on. Others don't necessarily need the supervision and micromanagement from others to accomplish what they've set out to do.

What happens when the first group of people don't have that kind of incentive to get work done? Procrastination ensues. You may think, at first, that now that you are in charge of your own reality, things are going to be different. But if you have no idea how to manage yourself, and you let your ego have free rein, you won't get far. No plan will work if you don't have the right progress-tracking tools to keep you accountable and in check.

8. Say no to what doesn't serve you

In Seneca's essay on tranquillity, he explains the Greek word euthymia as "believing in yourself and trusting that you are on the right path, and not being in doubt by following the myriad footpaths of those wandering in every direction." Even when you know exactly what it is you are pursuing, life tends to get in the way, distractions come to the surface and prevent you from following your intended trajectory, and you get side-tracked by other people or blinded by their own levels of success, you begin to compare your phase one to somebody else's phase ten.

Competitiveness is good when it is within certain bounds. It can push you to persevere, do your best, and give you all to your endeavours. However, the ego will take that competition and put a vicious twist on it, and then you begin to think that you have to be better than everybody else, that you have to surpass them in every way imaginable, that you have to have more wealth, more success, more possessions, more of everything than everyone. Because trust me, your ego always wants it all. So, you have to learn to say no, first of all, to your ego, then to outside distractions. You have to have an honest discussion with yourself, you must understand your priorities, and let go of anything that doesn't serve them.

9. Don't chase credit and recognition

Your ego feels too superior and entitled to actually do what many people describe as the grunt work. Even when you're starting out in a new pursuit, your ego often seeks short-term gratification, it wants to be the best at that thing instantly, and it wants you to believe that you have mastery over that venture even if you're not too familiar with what it entails.

The ego does not want to be left in the shadows, it craves recognition, validation, approval, and getting credit for its 'brilliance.' It does not deign to do the work that nobody else wants to do. It wants to rise in the ranks as quickly as possible. It tells you you're too experienced to be a novice, too old for a level entry job, too reputable for inconsequential tasks, and too knowledgeable for basic instructions.

If you prioritize this sense of entitlement, you will never get ahead. The same thing goes for refusing to submit to people who have proven to be experts in their fields. If you truly want to advance, you need to be willing to do the grunt work, but also to exchange short-term gratification for a long-term payoff.

10. If you find yourself in a hole, stop digging

Sometimes, when people find themselves in holes of their own making, they keep digging until they make it all the way to hell. If only they stopped and took the time to ask themselves: Is this the person who I want to be? Granted, everybody makes mistakes. Sometimes they have overly ambitious plans that are a bit too far-fetched. But because they feed their sense of grandiosity and ingenuity, they keep investing in those plans, even when the outcome is clearly unfavourable. They cannot get themselves to stop because they feel like they're in too deep. They already came this far, so the ego tells them they might as well see it through.

The ego does not want to admit failure, so it pushes them to dig even deeper until they hit rock bottom and they have no way of going back. What further fuels this issue is when you relate your entire identity to the work you do or the pursuit you're engaged in, so your ego tells you that any failure on your part will indicate to others just how bad of a person you are. It's in these times that mustering the courage to stop and not continue with the plunge becomes a turning point in your life. Despite how loud your ego screams or how wounded it feels, resist the urge to keep going, don't make things worse, take a moment to think, and plan.

11. Check your entitlement at the door

It doesn't matter if you're a millionaire or someone that snagged a good job and found success early on, that sense of certainty and entitlement that got you there will become a liability if you're not cautious with it. The ambitions that sustained your efforts and the goals and dreams that pushed you to work hard can easily turn into arrogance and pompousness when left unchecked.

The same goes for your sense of initiative and your ability to take charge. They can be a slippery slope to an addiction to control and power. Then when you feel compelled to prove the people who doubt you wrong, you're opening the gates to paranoia.

When your ego is entitled, it assumes that they've earned everything you have, and at the same time, it believes that your time and energy are more valuable than everyone else's. It overestimates your abilities to yourself, makes generous assumptions and judgments of your prospects, and produces ridiculous expectations, especially for others. This manifestation of your ego can lead to short-lived success but it eventually results in downright failure.

12. Focus on your higher purpose

We often get caught up in our own ideas of success, so much so that we construct these scenarios of what success is and what it looks like. These image games lead nowhere, especially when they're coming from your ego. The question here is not 'to be or not to be?' but as U.S. Air Force fighter pilot and Pentagon consultant John Boyd put it 'to be or to do?'

So, will you choose to get lost in your own fantasy of being successful? Will you obsess over the following you've amassed, what's in your bank account, your monthly pay-check, how many possessions you acquired, and the conquests you've had? Or will you choose to focus on a higher purpose?

In his book "Ego Is the Enemy," Ryan Holiday explains that "when we remove ego, we're left with what is real. What replaces ego is humility, yes—but rock-hard humility and confidence. Whereas ego is artificial, this type of confidence can hold weight. The ego is stolen. Confidence is earned. The ego is self-appointed, its swagger is artifice. One is girding yourself, the other gaslighting. It's the difference between potent and poisonous."

You know which way your ego wants to go, but which path do you want to follow?

Chapter Three:

What Would You Do If You Were Given One Year to Live?

If you were given only one year to live, what would you do?

Way back when I started writing this book my Dad asked what the book was about, after telling him he replied and said 'I would get a huge loan and go to Las Vegas and fuck it all!'. I don't even know if he can remember saying this, but I certainly can. It made me laugh. And to be fair, that's exactly what some of us might want to do! Although these were my Dad's words, this is not what I am suggesting, I thought to share as its funny, and yes the first part of this book is using the notion of having 'one year to live', but in actual fact its about making the most out of a year, hopefully carrying on with many more.

One year to live

It's such an emotionally charged question, so much so that when we ask ourselves what we would do if we were given only one year to live, our mind begins to race, contemplating everything from our fantasies and deepest desires to our paralyzing fears.

Truth be told, this question brings with it a whirlwind of possibility, but it also reminds us of everything we've put on hold. Suddenly, we're excruciatingly aware of how much we have forgotten and the panic begins to settle. How do we even approach the thought of our own death??

The future is in such a hurry to become the present as the present precipitates to dissolve into the past, and all we're left with is the everlasting regret of not doing enough. We slowly begin to realize that we have been absent, in a sense, from our lives, as events unfolded before our very eyes.

For the majority of it, despite our physical presence, we weren't fully there to experience the joy, or the sadness. While entirely conscious, we didn't embrace the present moment, nor did we allow ourselves to open our hearts completely.

We've had a few encounters where we were acutely aware of our feelings and those of the people surrounding us, but for the most part, we kept walking through life refusing to take off the impossibly burdensome shield weighing us down.

And, so instead of embracing the raw, wild, and exciting opportunities life brings our way, we're completely occupied by the armour we're wearing, whether people can see through the fortresses we've built, and whether we will need to draw our swords at any given moment.

We're so engulfed in what lies within that we don't take the time to understand or appreciate what is beyond our own existence. We're always at the ready, prepared to fight or bolt off before our defences corrode and wear away.

So, when faced with the one-year-to-live-your-life verdict, we begin to see how absent we've been throughout our lives, and how the only way to remedy that is to sharpen our focus and become more present. But how do we make sure we're fully alive and aware of ourselves as well as our surroundings each day?

It seems like such a challenging task, 'to be,' yet we're horrified at how unprepared we are. We fear that it may be too late for us, that we're not up for the task, and that any possibility to cram for our demise is far too ambitious. Our contemplation of this life and death-riddle brings with it a torrential downpour of questions, some fair, some reasonable, and some dubious or completely unsettling. With only one year left, there are numerous paths to consider.

Should we quit our job and pursue a whole other venture? Should we get married? Should we get divorced? Should we take up a new hobby? Should we get a piercing or a tattoo? Should we dye our hair a funky colour? Should we donate all of our belongings?

Should we discard our entire wardrobe and dress in a whole different aesthetic? Should we spend all of our hard-earned money on a lavish vacation, or should we leave it all to our heirs? Should we get plastic surgery, lose weight, get a personal trainer, and improve our physique? Should we go to therapy, enlist the council of a life coach, or hire a guru?

In my honest opinion, it all sounds like taking on more unfinished business than 'completing' our life cycle before we die. A death prognosis doesn't prompt one type of response only, there are as many plans of action as there are people and opinions. Your idea of what is worthwhile doesn't necessarily align with what another person may find fulfilling.

Journeys vary from one person to another, but the inevitability of death still remains. So, when considering what to do if you were given one year to live, you may keep your job, your family, and your friends, and focus instead on making the most out of your life as it currently is, meaning catering to your emotional, mental, and physical well-being without entirely uprooting your existence, or disturbing the balance you've come to establish.

There is no need to trade off all of your material but also intangible possessions for more pending projects if you're not entirely confident in your desire to engage in said projects. You may even feel fine with the current state of your life, give or take a few variables.

Perhaps you're seeking to nurture your spiritual side and focus on being more present and in the moment. Or maybe you'd like to find your purpose and pursue your passion in life, something which your career or personal obligations didn't allow you to do.

Either way, you can't afford to put working on fulfilling your lifelong dreams off for much time, because nobody knows when the first day of their final year begins. The truth is, some of us may not even have one whole year left to live, but the question is, why should we wait to get a terminal prognosis to finally start living a life that is true to our values and that honours who we are as individuals?

Maslow's Hierarchy of Needs

Maslow's hierarchy of needs is a motivational theory in psychology that consists of a five-tier model of human needs. This model often illustrates the five different stages as multiple levels in a pyramid. From the bottom and upwards, the hierarchical needs are the following: physiological needs, safety needs, belongingness and love needs, esteem needs, and self-actualization needs.

HIERARCHY OF NEEDS

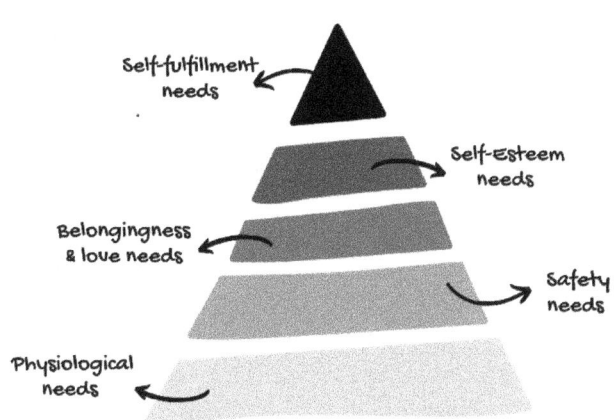

In order for individuals to tend to higher needs, they first must meet and fulfil needs that are lower in the hierarchy of the pyramid. The most basic human need is survival, so in this regard, survival is what motivates human behaviour first and foremost. Once that foundational requirement is fulfilled , the next level is what motivates the individual, and so on.

1. Physiological needs: These comprise essential biological requirements for human survival, including air, food, water, sleep, shelter, and warmth. If these needs go unfulfilled, the human body cannot function properly or at its optimal level. Maslow affirmed that physiological needs are the most important in the hierarchy, and all the other needs in the pyramid become secondary until these basic requirements are met.

2. Safety needs: Once a person's physiological needs are fulfilled, the needs for safety and security become salient. As human beings, we crave order and predictability in our lives. Granted, an adventurous spirit and spontaneity are great qualities to have, and they can be very useful, but for the most part, we thrive when we have a set routine. This allows us a sense of control over our lives with the possibility to spice things up every now and then. Safety and security needs are usually fulfilled by the family unit and society (schools, police, lawful institutions, business infrastructures, medical care, etc.).

3. Belongingness and love needs: After one's physiological and safety needs have been met, it's time to move to the third level in Maslow's hierarchy, which is belongingness and love. These needs are purely social in nature and

require building strong interpersonal relationships with others around us. This includes establishing friendships, trust, intimacy, and acceptance, as well as giving and receiving affection and love. In addition to that, belongingness requires that the person be part of or affiliated with a group (whether it be family, colleagues, friends, religion, ethnicity, etc.).

4. Esteem needs: Once the three initial requirements are met, Maslow's fourth level consists of esteem needs. In this tier, Maslow classified esteem into two different categories: (i) our esteem of ourselves -dignity, mastery, achievement, independence- and (ii) the esteem we seek from others, that is the respect and reputation we want - status, prestige, etc. It's noteworthy that the second type of esteem (i.e. respect and reputation) or validation in this context, is mainly sought after by children and adolescents, and thus, precedes self-esteem and dignity.

5. Self-actualization needs: This is the highest level in Maslow's hierarchy and refers to self-fulfilment, the realization of an individual's full potential, personal growth and development, as well as peak experiences. He describes this tier as the ambition to accomplish everything that an individual can so they can become the best version they can be. Many people focus on this need in particular because it's intrinsically linked to their goals in life, which is why the notion of self-actualization also differs from one person to the next. While the main premise remains unchanged, that is becoming the most one can become, the motivation varies. For instance, an

individual may have a strong desire to become a super parent, while another individual may want to become a renowned athlete, a great student, or an admirable business leader. Besides pursuing wealth or intelligence, this desire can also be expressed creatively, whether it's in writing, painting, photography, or inventions.

Maslow's hierarchy of needs aims to view the human experience from a more positive account, one that focuses on what can go right rather than what can go wrong. His theory is mainly interested in human potential and how we as people can fulfil that potential. Based on this understanding, self-actualization is not a destination we reach, it doesn't mean that once we are there, we're entitled to stay there for the remainder of our days. We're not static, on the contrary, we are always 'becoming' as individuals. Hence the need for personal growth and continuous discovery, because in self-actualization, we come across the things that are important to us and that give meaning to our lives. The level of self-actualization we're at can be measured through what Maslow called 'peak experiences.' Peak experiences occur when an individual experiences the world as it is, not as they think it ought to be. This can bring forth great feelings of joy, happiness, and wonder. With that in mind, it's important to note that this level is a never-ending process of self-fulfilment rather than an ideal state one achieves where they get their 'happily ever after.'

The 15 Traits of Self-Actualizers

As human beings, we often tend to stray away from fulfilling our potential when we regress to more primitive or aggressive behaviour. This, in part, is due to our path toward self-actualization being vague, untraced, or obstructed by misfortunes that disorient our true purpose.

You may be wondering how you got here in the first place, that, somehow, during the course of your life, you forgot how to live, you forgot to take pleasure in the small things, to be more present, to enjoy the moment, that somehow, you lost all of your spontaneity to make room for the familiar and predictable.

You may even be wondering why this wake-up call took so long, why you didn't take advantage of the time you've been given, spending it instead on the mundane and the trivial. A simple answer would be our survival instinct as human beings. Why do we pursue degrees? Why do we invest all of our time in unfulfilling jobs? Why do we do the things we do? It's taken me years to realise what I want out of life, it took bad things happening around me to kick my arse into gear.

Because we're seeking to meet our physiological and safety needs. We want comfort, we want shelter, and we want to be able to provide for ourselves and our families. Self-actualization is a luxury for most people, a concept they can't afford to think about as long as their basic needs aren't being met.

Unfortunately, consideration of one's true purpose almost always happens through tragedy, or when they're on their deathbed, which is why this one-year experiment is important. You don't have to be dying to finally realize you have neither fulfilled your dreams nor pursued your passion in life -though a that is good enough incentive.

For you to embark on this journey, you need to know where you want to end up, and what a life lived fully truly looks like, which is why you need to get to know the self-actualizer and his/her defining traits and qualities better.

The portrait of a self-actualized person is intricate and complex. And it's this ineffable intricacy and mystery of the human psyche that Maslow sought to understand. Though his approach focused on what can be done and what can improve rather than what cannot. In a way, Maslow can be considered as the founding father of the contemporary growth and self-development movement.

1. They perceive reality efficiently and embrace the unknown

Our relationship with reality is often ambiguous and intense, especially considering how encompassing reality is. Perhaps the number one fear or stressor of the human collective is the unknown, which is why we have several historic accounts explaining the unknowns of the past.

We have always tried to make sense of our surroundings, to banish uncertainty and replace it with the lucid, intelligible, and familiar. No matter how far-fetched those explanations and interpretations may be, we sleep better knowing we have the answers. Nobody likes an unsolved mystery.

We all want closure regardless of the means it takes to come to us or for us to get to it. But self-actualizing people are not afraid of the unknown and ambiguity. They don't shy away from tentativeness, doubt, and uncertainty, because what for us is torture, for them is a stimulating challenge, a rather high spot in life, not a low.

Self-actualizers are also able to detect dishonesty in people and generally have an accurate judgment of others. This extends to other aspects of life since they can see reality as what it is, unbiased and undisguised.

2. They accept themselves and others as they are

Acceptance is a major part of any healing journey. Whether it's accepting oneself for what one is or accepting others, flaws, weaknesses, and transgressions included. We're often overwhelmed by the amount of guilt, shame, and fear that overrides our thoughts and actions. We're crippled by anxieties and worries so much so that they begin to dictate the course of our lives.

But self-actualizing people aren't bridled by self-limiting beliefs. They're able to accept their human nature with all its imperfections, shortcomings, and disparity of the ideal image of what one ought to be.

This is not to say that they don't experience stress, fear, or guilt, they do but in adequate amounts and they don't give those feelings the power to take over their minds or obstruct their progress. The self-actualizer is also more in tune with their 'animal nature,' and isn't apologetic about fulfilling their desires in that sense.

3. They're spontaneous in thought and in action

Spontaneity is a quality that we tend to lose as we age. We chuck it down to impulsivity, a trait we wish to rid ourselves of. So, everything we do has to be thoroughly calculated in an attempt to anticipate all probable outcomes.

Surprises become less fun and more cause for concern. Through the routines we've built and the regimens we've established, we seek to completely eliminate the unpredictable as a way to stay ahead and on top of the trends.

We think of spontaneity as a form of naivety, too immature, too capricious, and childlike. We scoff at the unforeseeable discomfort, while deep down, we're envious of spontaneous people, of the people who can embark on adventures based on a simple whim, of the people who are able to voice their thoughts without thinking them over and over again.

In the world we live in, this is unconventional, for sure, but unconventionality in self-actualizers isn't meant to shock, vex, or disturb, on the contrary. Self-actualizers are highly critical and analytical thinkers.

They will go about conventional events and occurrences with grace and a good attitude, they will behave in a conventional fashion simply because it causes them no issues in particular. They won't waste their time fighting over trivialities with others. So, while spontaneous and unconventional, these people do not aim to offend, provoke, and antagonize their peers.

4. They're problem-centred

Self-actualized people are more problem-centred than ego-centred. They tend to focus on problems outside of themselves. In fact, they're not much concerned with themselves at all, unlike the obsessive introspectiveness we tend to develop during our teenage years.

They're highly effective at solving problems because they can detach their ego from the situation at hand when attempting to tackle a given issue. Generally speaking, they have a mission in life, a goal to accomplish, or a problem to solve which enlists the majority of their energy.

Because they know their 'why,' this instils them with a tremendous sense of purpose that allows them to work on tasks that they feel are their duty, responsibility, or obligation. Often, these tasks are nonpersonal, unselfish, or address the good of mankind. Your "why" is your strength. It's the power, the drive, and the passion that propels you forward. It's a constant that shapes every decision you make, big or small. As Simon Sinek put it in his book "Start with Why, "regardless of WHAT we do in our lives, our WHY—our driving purpose, cause or belief—never changes." — Simon Sinek, Start with Why

5. They're calm and enjoy privacy

Self-actualizers enjoy solitude and isolation to a greater degree compared to the average person. They can be solitary without feeling uncomfortable while alone with their thoughts. It's this isolation that allows them to focus on complex ideas, deep dive into their psyche, and develop a significant level of self-government, self-disciple, and self-decision.

With that said, this doesn't mean self-actualized individuals are antisocial by nature, but rather that they prefer to maintain a close circle of people around them, hence, they're not likely to invest their time in superficial relationships. Moreover, self-actualized people are often less flustered by outside stressors compared to other people.

They have the remarkable ability to remain calm and composed through difficult times, hardships, and misfortunes without resorting to violence or passive-aggressive behaviour. This is perhaps because they live according to their values and not those of other people so they're able to stick to their perception of events rather than rely on how others view the matter.

6. They're independent and autonomous

Self-actualized people are not dependent on people, culture, or their environment for satisfaction. Because they're motivated by the promise of growth rather than the fear of deficiency, the self-actualizer is dependent on their own development and continuous improvement of their potential.

In this sense, they're autonomous active agents that are able to maintain their serenity when facing what makes other people uncomfortable. While not caring about other people's thoughts and opinions might seem like an act of rebellion, this is not the case for self-actualization.

Building proper boundaries that ensure your independence from the disorienting and superfluous opinions of others is perhaps the only way to not only preserve your sanity but find fulfilment in the things you do.

When you're not swayed by the worries that the people around you will find your passion pointless, absurd, or insignificant, you're free to pursue your dreams because they're meaningful to you, and that's the only thing that should matter.

7. They can freshly enjoy things (as if it were the first time)

Gratitude is a virtue that we tend to lose the older we grow, and so throughout the course of time, as we navigate the twists and turns of life, we begin to forget how paramount gratitude is, especially in appreciating the little, yet immensely beautiful, things.

A death prognosis (although hypothetical) will allow you to experience the beauty of the sunset, flowers, trees and greenery, and the crisp morning air, as you would have for the first time. It's only when we realize we have very little time left that we realize how many things we took for granted.

The self-actualizer can freshly enjoy things as if they were seeing/feeling/ and experiencing them for the very first time. For these individuals, even casual workdays and moment-to-moment ventures can be exciting, thrilling, and enchanting.

This 'newness' is a very child-like perception in nature, it boasts a certain degree of playfulness, a refreshing view of a world that never seems to go dull. Moreover, this is a quality that allows you to appreciate the basic goods of life, again and again, no matter how stale or repetitive these experiences may have become to others.

8. They have peak experiences that transcend the ordinary

The loss of self and relinquishing control can allow significant revelations -about how we perceive our different experiences and the world as a whole- to sprout and come to the surface. There's nothing more freeing than the mystical experience of throwing off the chains, ripping off the veil over our eyes, and shattering the excruciating awareness of mortality.

This transcendence from the ordinary to the sublime or divine heightens the intensity of your feelings so you begin to experience the world around you to the fullest extent. The different catalysts of such experiences range from art, literature, music, and sexual intimacy, and extend to any situation that involves loss of self, meditation, and acute concentration.

9. They're concerned for the welfare of humanity

Self-actualizers have a deep sense of community and are committed to the welfare of humanity. They have a vision that is much bigger than themselves and experiences a deep feeling of identification and sympathy for other human beings.

Because of this, they feel inclined to help others despite being distant or alienated from societal conventions.

The truth is, we all have a need for identification, belonging, and affection. We want to be part of something bigger than us, whether it be a group of people, a cause, or an idea. This is often what gives meaning to our daily endeavours and what motivates us to get up in the morning. It is this need that fuels our purpose and drives our pursuit of the greater good.

10. They have deeper interpersonal relationships with a few people

Self-actualized people tend to have very few close friends and acquaintances. Their social circles are usually small because they're highly selective of the people they choose to surround themselves with. Despite their limited social network, or perhaps thanks to it, they have deeper bonds with the people in their lives and seek to continuously nurture the interpersonal relationships they've built.

They seek deeper and more profound connections, they're also capable of greater affection and identification. Furthermore, they find no issue in speaking realistically and sometimes sternly to the people who deserve it, especially hypocrites and egoists.

11. They have democratic attitudes

Self-actualized individuals have a democratic character structure and don't discriminate in their relationships with others. They can be friendly to anyone regardless of their social status, race, education, political beliefs, religion, etc. As a matter of fact, self-actualizers often seem unaware of these factors of differentiation.

To demonstrate such an attitude and proclivity to judge people based on their character and not their status or ethnicity requires a certain degree of humility and pure virtue. This respect for other people is simply because they are fellow human beings is a fundamental constituent of self-actualization.

12. They have strong moral and ethical standards

Self-actualizing people have definite ethical standards and strong morals. Their notions of good and evil, though not entirely conventional, are categorical and rarely put them in a situation where they have to debate whether an action/ decision is right or wrong.

Moreover, they're aware of the limits that separate good from evil and moral from immoral and hence choose to orient themselves in accordance with that idea. The same is applicable to their notion of means and ends, as most of the time, self-actualizers are entrenched in doing more than the outcome and value both equally.

13. They have a non-hostile sense of humour

While humour is a debatable topic that stirs many opinions, especially when it's at the expense of someone else, which implicitly communicates a certain level of hostility, self-actualizing people have a more straightforward sense of humour that isn't aimed at targeting and hurting another person's feelings.

Their sense of humour is almost philosophical, directed at humanity as a whole as well as its shortcomings. This can take many forms, including poking fun at themselves, not in a self-deprecating or masochistic way, but more in a functional or constructive manner.

14. They're creative

Creativity for the self-actualized doesn't necessarily entail artistic and imaginative ventures like art, music, and literature. Creativity is a quality that elevates any activity or line of work simply based on the attitude of the person involved.

In this context, one can be a creative carpenter, plumber, shoemaker, accountant, or even clerk just because they can project a genuine expression of themselves and their personalities into the world. Accordingly, there is no limit to the extent one can engage in creative endeavours. So that whatever a person does, they do so with an attitude and a spirit that stems directly from the nature of the person's character who is performing the act.

This occurs when the person isn't inhibited by what other people think or how they view their actions, which brings about a certain freedom akin to spontaneity. This quality is closely related to what Maslow called "the universal creativeness of unspoiled children", which allows anyone to find joy in the most mundane and monotonous of tasks.

15. They're resistant to enculturation (but they're not purposely unconventional)

The whole world is engaged in a perennial attempt to impose norms and traditions on its individuals, and so it is the duty of the self-actualized to question those norms and put them under scrutiny. While they do get along with the dominant culture in more than one way, they still resist enculturation and favour inner detachment from the culture in which they're immersed.

This isn't an account of going against the grain to make a rebellious statement, but rather that aims to prevent cultural imperatives from defining their reality. So, they don't allow themselves to be passive and reactive instead of active and responsive.

Self-actualizing people don't want popular opinion to dictate their decisions, or determine what they see as good and what they see as bad. It's worth mentioning that they neither accept everything they're presented with like a sheep nor do they reject everything like the typical rebel. Instead, they let their self-decision, autonomy, and code of ethics guide their choices and behaviour.

Despite all this, self-actualized individuals are not perfect. Self-actualization is not an end, it's rather a mechanism, a tool, an intellectual, moral, and intuitive compass that aims to direct you towards a more fulfilling and meaningful life. There are no perfect human beings, and you shouldn't aim for perfection either because that's only a delusion. Instead, use self-actualization as what it is, a vision for growth, self-development, and continuous improvement.

The Power of Intention

Most people are impatient when it comes to change so they want to see results quickly. We've all been guilty of this, taking the crash diet approach (I think I'm currently on my 1500th one), swinging between two separate states of 'all or nothing.' While there's no harm in wanting to enjoy the fruits of your labour, if you don't allow them enough time to bloom and ripen, there won't be much for you to enjoy.

Patience is key because all good things take time. More importantly, all good things take some work. You're ready to put in the effort, but where do you even begin? The answer is, with intention. If you want to make the most out of the year you've been given, then you can't let the winds of circumstance dictate the direction your life is headed.

Yes, you're happy when there's reason to be, and yes, you're sad or angry when faced with a displeasing situation, but for the most part (which is the reason why you're in this place right now), you have allowed whatever happened in your life to guide where you were headed. The issue with this is that you're placing your fate in the hands of frantic forces.

While there are many things that lie beyond your control, things that you should learn to simply accept as they come, there are also many aspects of your life that you can control through the power of intention. As Wayne Dyer put it, "Our intention creates our reality." Science tells us that we tend to walk in the direction we're facing.

We also steer the wheel and, by extension, the car, where we're gazing. In the same way, the thoughts we allow to take control are the ones that guide the course of our lives. In this regard, we can set our intention either to prepare ourselves for success or for failure. So, when we focus our mental energy on one particular goal, we automatically allow more brain power to fuel that desire.

Subsequently, with the mind placed in the right position, it's able to perform much more efficiently to make that intention a reality. With that said, you can't do this just once, forget about it, and expect consistent results. Your efforts in setting your intentions should be continuous.

In a way, you will be creating a mental vision board that guides your every thought and action, keeping you accountable and motivated all at the same time. There are three necessary steps that will allow you to harness the power of intention while you work on the mental, physical, emotional, and spiritual sides of your one-year-to-live journey.

1. Decide what you want

Your intentions need to be clear and concise. Whether you're seeking personal or professional development and growth, you have to know exactly what you're aiming for. There are many ways to use the power of intention for goal setting. The traditional SMART goals entail that these are specific, measurable, achievable, realistic, and time-bound. But, this approach doesn't work for everyone. It's not ideal because you can easily forget about those goals until it's time to review your progress. You might get confused about the differences between what is achievable and what is realistic. The 'measurable' aspect can also be boring if you're not that data-focused.

While the SMART goals method can get the job done, it's somewhat archaic and ill-fitting for your one-year plan. The goal-setting approach you choose should include an assessment that allows you to track your progress as you go. Ideally, it should also create opportunities for feedback. When you have expectations laid out, this can push you to maintain the pace needed so you can meet those expectations.

A great addition to SMART goals is the DUMB goals methodology. The acronym stands for dream-driven (are you being ambitious?), uplifting (is your goal positive and energizing?), method-friendly (can it be broken into simple routines?), and behaviour-driven (can you harness the power of habit?). A combination of the two with some additional steps here and there can make your goal-setting a lot more effective. If you would like to get a good flavour on DUMB goals and understand them better go over to YouTube and watch a video from Brendon Burchard - How NOT to Set Goals (Why S.M.A.R.T. goals are lame). Brendon nails the whole concept of DUMB goal setting. And please, don't get put off by the name of this acronym, it's not Dumb!

DUMB GOALS

- **D** — DREAM-DRIVEN — Are you being ambitious?
- **U** — UPLIFTING — Is your goal positive and energising?
- **M** — METHOD-FRIENDLY — Can it be broken in to simple routines?
- **B** — BEHAVIOUR-DRIVEN — Can you harness the power of habit?

To get started, you need to take a deep dive into your psyche to better understand yourself, what motivates you, what is important to you, etc. Without this knowledge, you might set the wrong goals simply because they sound nice on paper, or because other people are also setting those goals. Your goals need to be your own, based on your core values and your priorities. After some much-needed self-exploration, you can move on to brainstorming to create a list of possible goals.

Don't rush this process, take your time while collecting ideas, and step away from the list if need be so you can come back to it with a fresh perspective. Once you have a list of potential objectives, it's time to filter and prioritize.

Ask yourself: is this aligned with my values? Is this worth my time? Is this relevant to where and how I see myself in a year's time? Is this worth the sacrifice? Is this sustainable? Imagine your future once you have achieved this goal but also your future without having achieved this goal. What does your life look like? How different would it be? Are you excited about that future?

If the difference is negligible then you should reconsider how worthwhile that goal is. So, remember to plan proactively, visualize the way, break things down, use the power of habit, focus on building efficient systems, reflect frequently, and fully commit to no zero days (meaning you have to do one task every single day that will bring you closer to your goal(s)).

2. Identify your 'why'

"Our visions are the world we imagine, the tangible results of what the world would look like if we spent every day in pursuit of our WHY." Simon Sinek – Start with Why

Why do you want to achieve the goals you determined? You may believe you want to make a career change, travel the world, take an extended vacation, start a business, or join a non-profit organization. But, why? What will those objectives get you and how will they make you feel? This is important to consider because you want to make sure that you're pursuing the things you are for a good reason. Identifying your 'why' also gives power to your intention.

3. Visualize where you want to be

When you know what you want and why you want it, you also have a clearer idea of where you're headed and how to get there. The first two steps lay the groundwork for your intention, while visualization helps you plan for the future and map out a detailed path to help you reach your destination.

Visualization is also powerful because it allows you to live the future you want in the present moment, getting you that much closer to making your dreams a reality.

With this knowledge in mind, you can move on to address the various aspects of your life (mental, physical, emotional, and spiritual).

The Wheel of Life Assessment

If you are into personal growth and development, you might already be familiar with the wheel of life and what it represents. On the other hand, if you're just dipping your toes in the pool of self-improvement, this might be a new concept for you. While I am not reinventing the wheel in this case (no pun intended), I do believe in the valuable insights this assessment can offer.

This assessment goes hand in hand with the death meditation and epitaph writing exercises in the first chapter. Completing those two should have given you a better idea of what you really want in life, and completing this one will show you how the current state of the different aspects of your life aligns with your aspirations. Any discrepancies are indicative of areas you need to work on.

I can confidently say that it has been successful not only for myself but also for my clients. This is aimed to help you identify and gain perspective. Though I do want to note that if you haven't dropped your ego yet, then the information you fill out will most likely be disingenuous. This will nullify the results you get and the exercise simply won't work.

The wheel of life is a tool that can help you assess how balanced your life currently is. Although the perfect balance between all aspects cannot be achieved, sometimes, one aspect of your life can require most of your energy and time, which means other aspects can suffer from this, so you may feel as if your life is out of control. The wheel of life can help you gain some perspective and identify the areas that need some tending. To create your personal wheel of life, you need to examine your satisfaction in the following areas.

The Mental

- Contribution: Giving back to the community, charity work, contributions to society …
- Growth: Personal growth, learning, self-development, career fulfilment, personal and professional achievements.

The Physical

- Wealth: Financial stability, future growth in wealth, and income that satisfies your current needs.
- Health: Physical health, satisfaction with your level of fitness, efforts to maintain your well-being through sleep, exercise, and eating habits.

The Emotional

- Romantic relationship: Responsible, intimate, and loving relationship.
- Relationships with friends and family: Getting along with your family, having a trustworthy circle of

friends, making the most of the time you spend with your friends, etc.

The Spiritual

- Relationship with the self: Self-respect, self-acceptance, self-love, healthy self-esteem.
- Connection with the spiritual: Spiritual guidance, connection with the inner and outer world, and healthy relationship with your spiritual being.

1) On a scale of 1 to 10 (where 1 represents very low satisfaction and 10 represents very high satisfaction) rate your satisfaction with each aspect of the wheel of life. This doesn't mean the time and energy you spend on each area, but rather how satisfied you are with the quality of that category.

___ Contribution
___ Growth
___ Wealth
___ Health
___ Relationship with friends and family
___ Romantic relationship
___ Relationship with self
___ Connection with the spiritual

2) Use the circle graph in the book to fill your rating for each category (0 being the centre and 10 being the extremity).

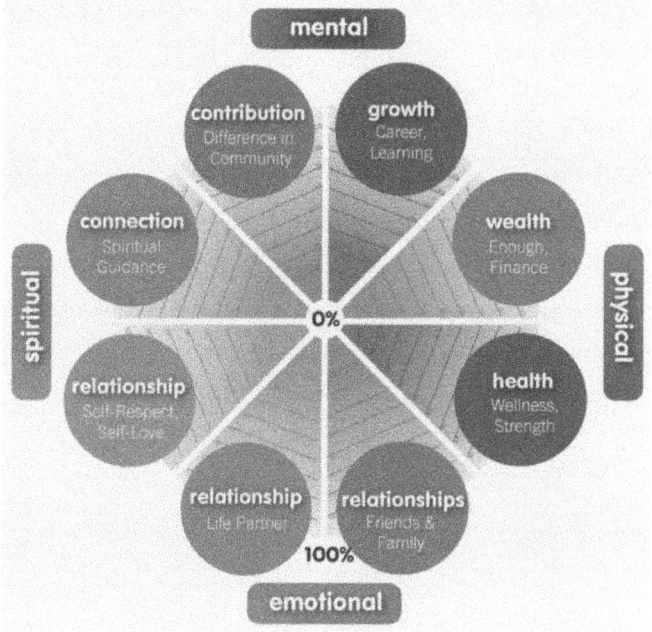

Now answer the following questions.

- How balanced is your wheel?
- What area in your life are you most wanting/willing to make a difference in?
- What is the current state of this area?
- What do you feel is missing or not working out in this aspect?
- What is your ideal score for each category that you want to achieve in a year's time?
- Where are the biggest gaps in your satisfaction levels?
- What actions do you need to take to address those gaps?
- What does success look like (for you) in each respective area?

3) Now that you have completed your wheel of life, it's time to take some action. For each area that you feel needs improvement, write down three key goals that will help you improve and bring more balance to your life. These could be as ambitious as starting a business or as simple as checking up on your friends more regularly -whatever you feel passionate about.

Side note: While I can't necessarily push you to do anything, my aim here is to guide you while you work on achieving the goals you've set for yourself. I can only specify, explain, and demonstrate, so it's up to you to follow through with this.

Mental

Goal 1

_____

_____

Goal 2

_____

_____

Goal 3

_____

_____

Physical

Goal 1

_____

_____

Goal 2

_____

_____

Goal 3

_____

_____

Emotional

Goal 1

_____

_____

Goal 2

_____

_____

Goal 3

_____

_____

Spiritual

Goal 1

_____

_____

Goal 2

_____

_____

Goal 3

_____

_____

Chapter four:

What Is Your Plan?

Life is unpredictable, and you cannot be certain that you will have the mental, physical, and emotional ability to do all the things you want to do in the distant future. For many people, it takes a serious illness, hitting retirement age, or a major life-altering event for them to begin thinking about all the things they want to do before they die.

This book is meant to give you a head start in that regard, so it's not too late for you to turn your dreams into a reality. You can't keep waiting for the 'perfect' time to do so, if anything, a bucket list is essential not because you're dying but because you want to experience the joys of being alive.

It's really about living life to the fullest with all the days you have left, so that on your deathbed, you're filled with contentment, relief, and happiness for all you've accomplished, not regret for all that's been left unsaid and undone. Although regrets are a natural part of life, there are some that could easily be nullified or lifted by action. In Bronnie Ware's critically acclaimed 2012 book, inspired by her time as a palliative carer, "The Top Five Regrets of The Dying", she explains "life is over so quickly. It is possible to reach the end with no regrets. It takes some bravery to live it right, to honour the life you are here to live but the choice is yours... Appreciate the time you have left by valuing all of the gifts in your life and that includes especially, your own, amazing self."

Your One Year to Live Bucket List

Often, when people think of the term bucket list, they envision these earth-shattering aspirations. Perhaps it's touring the six continents in under a year, climbing the highest mountain, quitting their jobs and going on a spiritual journey, becoming a Buddhist monk, or getting lost in the wilderness.

While thrill seeking has its special place in many people's hearts, including my own, this doesn't mean a bucket list isn't truly one if it doesn't involve drastic experiences. I use the term bucket list because it's the closest description to your 'one year to live' prognosis. 'Smaller' goals can be just as rewarding. The truth is, it all depends on who you are as a person and what you aspire to be.

What may be meaningful to you may not bring as much satisfaction to another person and vice versa. This is why self-exploration is essential. It allows you to anticipate and eventually prevent regrets that would only cause you anguish when it's too late to act. For instance, most people regret not spending enough time with their families and loved ones. This is just one of the many areas that you are likely to agonize over when the time comes. Not that you necessarily will, but you have to take yourself there right this moment, you have to consider the possibility. I am sharing this as an example of the many potential regrets you want to consider with this next part.

To create a compelling bucket list, you need to venture deep into your mind and reflect on the things you hold in high regard, as well as those you don't care much for.

With this in mind, you want to take the concept of a bucket list, combine it with what you aim to achieve and apply the 'one year to live' notion to those goals and aspirations. And much like any worthwhile life endeavour, balance is key. Below are the necessary steps to follow that will guide you through crafting your one year to live bucket list.

Step 1: Write it down

Studies show that people are much more successful in achieving their goals when they write them down and/or share them with others -mainly because this provides them with a sense of accountability.

So, for the first step of creating your bucket list, you need to decide where you're going to store it. You can use a notebook, a Word document, an Excel sheet, an app, or a personal blog/ website. Whatever helps you categorize your goals into different sections, based on the wheel of life assessment you took previously (mental, physical, emotional, and spiritual).

Having your goals in writing can help you clear all the mind clutter from the endless inner monologues and organize your thoughts in a more structured and methodical way. Moreover, identifying all the things you want to do and putting them in writing can get you one step closer to figuring out an action plan that will allow you to accomplish those objectives.

Step 2: Pick a number of goals/aspirations

While the length of your one-year-to-live according to the bucket list is solely up to you, you should aim for goals that expand over different aspects of your life and with varying degrees of difficulty. There is no magic number, but mixing in some small or short-term goals that can easily be achieved will give you a sense of accomplishment and help keep you motivated for the ones that may require a lot of hard work, time, and long-term commitment.

In addition to that, when you continuously put in the effort to complete those objectives, you will begin to assimilate the sense of achieving as a habit to maintain. While this isn't a conventional bucket list (since a conventional one entails that your lifetime is the deadline), all of your goals should have a fixed date for accomplishment.

Setting deadlines creates a sense of urgency which will help you overcome procrastination and avoid pushing your goals further and further into the future with the excuse that 'you will get to them eventually.' In the context of having only a year to live, your ultimate deadline for these goals is evidently one year. Some of those objectives you might accomplish months ahead, but for the most part, your plans shouldn't extend beyond that one year you've been given.

Some goals will be harder to complete than others, and you most likely will have to push yourself outside of your usual comfort zone. With that in mind, you should also be realistic with your deadlines.

You can be ambitious with what you aim to accomplish but you should also account for challenges and setbacks, so allowing yourself some wiggle room will help you stay on course and keep track of your progress. A great way to avoid losing momentum is to break down your bigger goals into smaller and more achievable ones. So, within your ultimate one-year to live bucket list, you can have mini-lists that don't seem as daunting as that one monstrous objective you've been putting off for years.

Step 3: Dig deeper for ideas

When making a bucket list, you're bound to have a number of items in the forefront of your mind, things you've always wanted to try, places you've always wanted to visit, people you've always wanted to meet, or those in your life you would like a second chance with, perhaps to apologize, make amendments, and reconnect, behaviours you would want to change, etc...

You can start by writing those down to help you clear some space in your head. Once you've done that, it's time to come up with other incredible and creative ideas. Compartmentalizing your life into a list of various categories

What Is Your Plan?

(i.e., the wheel of life) can make the brainstorming process much faster and easier. This is also a more convenient way to organize your list once it starts to grow.

Take your notebook and start a new page, divide it into all the different categories and make five entries for each one. Some goals may fit into more than one group in particular but that shouldn't be an issue as long as you record them. Below is a list of sections you can use/ consider when creating your own.

- Career and Finance
- Charity/Contribution
- Education
- Personal growth
- Family and kids
- Creativity
- Entertainment
- Events
- Local experiences
- Sports and activities
- Food and drink
- Travel
- Nature and wildlife
- Adventure
- Just for fun

Ask yourself these 26 questions (don't allow your fear to guide your answers, this is the time to dream bigger!).

1. Are there any activities or sports that you want to try?

2. If money and fear were not an issue what would you do?

3. What are some of your childhood dreams or goals that you were never able to fully explore but you still find enticing?

4. If you had three wishes what would they be?

5. If you were on your deathbed, what would be your regrets?

6. If you could be remembered for three things, what would they be?

7. If you won the lottery today, what would you do?

8. In what ways do you want to improve yourself physically, mentally or spiritually?

9. Is there a charity you have always wanted to support?

10. What would your ideal day look like?

11. What activities have you done in the past that you really enjoy and find fulfilling?

12. If you could start all over again with your life, what would you do differently?

13. Is there someplace you have always wanted to take your partner, best friend, or parent?

14. What classes have you always thought about taking?

15. What cultural traditions are you interested in?

16. What events do you want to attend?

17. What has always been your biggest dream in life?

18. What skills have you wanted to learn?

19. What travel and adventure stories would you want to share with your grandchildren?
20. When you imagine yourself as really, really relaxed and happy, what are you doing?
21. What types of new foods do you want to try?
22. What would you do now if you knew that you wouldn't fail?
23. What was your childhood dream, and is it still relevant today?
24. What would you like to do with your family and friends?
25. Where in the world would you like to go?
26. Who have you always wanted to meet in person?

These questions have allowed you to venture deep inside your mind to find the experiences you're most passionate about. Now you can start cultivating ideas from the outer world. Once you're in the right mindset, your brain will be on high alert whenever an interesting spot, experience, or activity are mentioned.

Step 4: Finalize your bucket list (and prep for execution)

There is no right or wrong way of making your bucket list, there isn't a set format or template to follow, no specific prescription either. This is a personal journey that reflects your aspirations and what you desire the most in life, which means it's different from one person to the next.

The key element here is to come up with entries that are meaningful to you and items that will inspire you to get up each morning with a spark in your eyes and a fire in your heart. Your goals and aspirations don't have to be ground-breaking, or thrill-seeking.

Sometimes the most minimalistic goals can be the most gratifying (like donating blood for instance). With that said, don't exclude any items out of fear of failure or sheer discomfort. Also, don't exclude any items that you think are too small or too insignificant!

As long as it's meaningful to you, then it should be on your list. A bucket list is meant to stretch your comfort zone, and as cheesy as it sounds, often what matters the most is the journey rather than the destination.

Now that you know how to create a bucket list, you can move on to creating an action plan that targets each one of your goals. Below are a few examples of how you can approach certain aspects of your life that are in dire need of change (for instance, finding purpose, making a career change, catering to your mental health, etc.)

The Wheel of Life – The 4 Aspects of Self-improvement

Every choice you make shapes your future. Every decision you take determines the direction your life is going to take. We may not think about this very often. But the small or insignificant details matter just as much as the substantial ones. This fact is kind of hard to swallow, isn't it? Many would prefer to think that what they are is a by-product of their environment, and so they refuse to take any accountability for their decisions and choices.

After all, it's much easier to believe you're a victim of circumstances than to see yourself as an acting agent whose patterns of behaviour carry tremendous impact. Because then you don't really have to act, you're just going with the flow wherever it may take you. However, if there is one lesson to take from your "one year to live" prognosis it's that the choices you make create your reality.

They are far more important than your abilities or your circumstance. Let's say you have an unpleasant boss who constantly criticizes you and what you do. Their negative comments are so frequent, insulting, and often unsolicited that you begin to doubt your ability to perform your job. In this situation, you have two options, either you choose to believe your boss and what they say, or you decide to trust yourself and your aptitudes.

Think about the way you react when other people try to make you feel small and inadequate. Why are you allowing yourself to give them that much power? What about your qualities and traits? What role do they play in defining who you are? Does your level of education play a role in that too? Does it limit what you think you can or cannot do? That, too, is a choice.

For instance, you may not deem yourself smart enough to earn a higher degree or apply for a better position. But how much truth does that hold? Is that an accurate assessment or did you simply choose not to do the work because it's too demanding?

There are many ways to expand your horizons and acquire new skills and knowledge. Most importantly, they don't all require a hefty financial investment or an anxiety-inducing entrance exam. Have you ever explored the depths of your talents to identify where your proclivities lie?

Your assignment for this section is to closely observe your choices. You need to examine your own process of decision-making and evaluate the what, the why, and the how. Analyse every decision you make, from the food you put into your body to the amount of time you dedicate to various tasks, to the people you surround yourself with. Do the choices you make inhibit you or do they nurture your growth?

Below, we will examine how you can cater to the four main categories of the wheel of life so you can live your best life mentally, physically, emotionally, and spiritually.

The Mental

On the surface level, the mind represents our thought patterns and how our mind operates. On a deeper level, it consists of our beliefs, desires, values, and aspirations. The beliefs we hold are the opinions and convictions we take as truths without necessarily having immediate proof. Values, on the other hand, represent what we believe to be most important in different aspects of our lives.

The values and beliefs we hold often stem from the thoughts that were formed very early in our childhood. Every one of us has a deep desire to acquire or achieve something in our lives. This is the main reason why we set goals and intentions to help us get to where we want to be. Our thoughts can generate those goals or desires, so in a way, they direct our mental focus towards efforts and actions that sustain our objectives. This is how our minds learn and process everything around us. It's also one of the main aspects of ourselves that we are most familiar with.

When the thoughts on the surface level come into contact with our emotional side, they often collide with the baggage we've accumulated over the course of our existence. This, in turn, may create some turbulence. This baggage is deeply rooted in the fears we've internalized in the past, which can project into the present and the future causing some worry and anxiety. It can also come from hostile experiences that result in festering anger and resentment whether it's toward someone or a particular situation. This generates a pattern that triggers our bitterness and causes us to respond with anger when similar conditions recur.

Practices for Mental Wellness

Exercise your mind:

Your thought patterns, beliefs, and values greatly influence your psychological well-being. You can't let go of those self-limiting beliefs and you can't defeat your ego if the tools at your disposal are dull and unsharpened. Your mind can be your worst enemy just as it can be your greatest ally. It all depends on what you feed it and how you take care of it. Depending on your results per the previous chapter's wheel of life assessment, you may be neglecting the mental aspect. If that's the case then you need to map a plan that will bring more balance to your wheel, and by extension, your life. Completing a mentally challenging activity early in the day benefits the mind just like physical activity benefits the body. It's a strengthening workout that keeps your mind sharp and prepares it to face the cognitive demands of the day. Setting aside a part of your morning routine for a mental challenge takes up very little of your time and is a small intellectual investment that goes a long way.

Invest in something you've always wanted to learn:

The point of having one year to live is you get the opportunity to reassess your life choices and how closely they align with your lifelong wish or dream. It's a chance for you to gauge how far you've come and determine where you would like to be. In this regard, there has to be something you've always wanted to learn but have never found the time for due to your daily obligations and preoccupations. You simply cannot afford to wait for your next vacation to learn a new skill. Now is the time to take action and set yourself on the path to your desired destination. So, make sure your "one year to live" plan takes this element into account. No matter how inexperienced you are, you can still learn a little each day all while working at a comfortable pace. We all start somewhere, what's most important is that you're progressing each time towards a new skill that you've always wanted to acquire. You will have learned something you've always wanted to before you even know it, and from then on, you can move to the next learning goal in your continuous self-improvement journey.

The Physical

The physical component of your wheel of life consists of health (strength and wellness) and wealth (finance and fulfilment). But even within this category, there could be an imbalance. For instance, you might have reached financial stability but your physical health is not optimal. Sometimes you may even sacrifice one for the other. The objective of this assessment is to examine which categories are lacking in wellness and remedy that.

Your physical body reflects who you are. It's the total sum of everything that makes you, you. Your body is a barometer of sorts; one that indicates how things are going in all the different areas of your existence. Healthy eating habits and a good exercise regimen are typically what come to mind when people think about strength and physical wellness.

With that said, your workout routine isn't the only thing to consider when looking to improve your health. In fact, we all know people who follow clean diets, and while they are physically fit, they still carry an excessive amount of mental and emotional stress. Although this may not be immediately recognizable, chronic stress can take a tremendous toll on your health.

Stress usually occurs when our mental, physical, emotional, and spiritual needs are not being met. When it does, this triggers the fight-flight response, a survival mechanism that is hard-wired into our genetic composition. This response is how our physiology prepares us to react to what could potentially be a life-threatening event. So, when it's triggered continuously, that response generates further distress and anxiety.

Strength and physical wellness are much more than the mere absence of disease. We are in optimal health when we are able to maintain harmony between each of the four aspects of our lives (mental, physical, emotional, and spiritual). While the physical body represents the foundation that everything else is built upon in our lives, it is equally important to exercise each of the other three aspects on a regular basis as well. So, we must set our individual health, fitness, and wellness regimens. In my opinion, and from experience achieving harmony in life cannot happen if these four categories aren't balanced and in accordance with one another.

Practices for Physical Wellness

Do a little resistance training:

Resistance training is a type of exercise that involves exerting your muscles to their maximum performance. While cardiovascular activity, namely walking, is certainly beneficial to your health, resistance training, comes with the added benefit of toning your muscles and boosting your metabolism. Even simple resistance exercises like climbing up the stairs or doing push-ups can help you get stronger and more in shape in a few sessions.

Replace unhealthy options with your favourite fruits and vegetables:

Replacing your junk food drawer (or cupboard if we're being more realistic) can be a painful experience. Parting with the scrumptious processed snacks for bland healthy alternatives is a sacrifice you're not entirely sold on making. Besides, the two don't seem to even compare in terms of flavour. However, when you have only one year to live, it certainly puts things in perspective. Suddenly, all those small details you would usually spend hours at a time obsessing over don't matter anymore. You most likely have your own favourite fruits and vegetables, so why not try to incorporate them into your diet and at the same time replace the unhealthy alternatives? I know the obvious answer to that question is "Fuck it!", "I only have one year to live so who cares? I am going to enjoy myself and indulge in some good food because I deserve it!" While I agree with you on that and I urge you to take pleasure in the things that make you happy, I have to add that -as you've probably heard many times before, moderation is key. And please don't think of me as some kind of saint, or physical specimen, I'm really not! I do what I can, I have my good days and bad, just like everyone else.

The Emotional

We live in a world of commodities, and while wealth and financial stability are important, they're not everything. Most people, when hypothetically given one year to live, choose to work on their personal lives, engage in meaningful ventures, and seek fulfilment rather than accumulate more money and possessions.

The truth is our pursuit of the material stems from the dominant cultural narrative that continuously tries to convince us we're not enough, and that happiness comes from material objects. The problem with this way of thinking is that no matter how much money we have and no matter how many things we own, there will always be something better. This makes objects lose their appeal as soon as we acquire them.

But happiness does not come from the outside, it rather comes from within. Fulfilment can only come through witnessing your own growth and how far you're willing to go since you've received your hypothetical death prognosis.

The goal of having one year to live is so that in the final days, when you hit pause and contemplate the substantial changes you've made in your life, you're able to feel a sense of meaning and purpose, that your efforts were worth it, that they were not in vain.

This will be a long process, and at times, an arduous one, but it also will be most rewarding. At the current moment, you may feel overwhelmed as you're trying to manage day-to-day struggles. You may even have fallen into the mentality that other people's lives are much more interesting than your own. Perhaps this is the reason why you picked up this book. You're in desperate need of change and you're ready to make the commitment.

These thoughts are further fuelled by social media, especially when we're constantly bombarded by an endless stream of pictures and videos from other people leading the "perfect" life. But the thing is, everything you see in that bubble is not a reflection of the reality those people live in.

Those are merely highlighting from the experiences they've had. They're only showcasing the good in an active attempt to suffocate the bad and the ugly. On some level of thought, we're aware of this, yet every time we get a notification that one of our friends posted a video from an exotic island showing off their dream vacation haven, we're envious of how magical their life is.

While seeking fun adventures and travel is a great way to enrich your life and add to your experiences, fulfilment should first and foremost be generated from within. It's about staying focused on what moves you, finding what sparks your passion, and creating experiences of all different kinds, because that is what makes life meaningful. Finding your joie de vivre (joy of living) may take some time, perhaps even some research and development on your part, but it will be rewarding.

Practices for Emotional Wellness

Stop waiting for that magic moment to save you

Many people waste the majority of their lives waiting for that magic moment to manifest, thinking that one day, they will have the sudden realization of what they're meant to do with their lives, that inspiration will strike and infuse them with a sense of purpose, that suddenly everything will make sense, and they will be able to view their past experiences as all these blocks that have fallen into place, preparing them for their ultimate destination.

Inspiration is not to be trusted, so they're left hanging, stuck in the same spot years, sometimes decades down the line. Waiting and passivity, are enemies of passion and determination. The truth is, you can't sit around waiting for that magic moment when everything in your life suddenly clicks. That's a rare (if even possible) occurrence. If you want to discover your life's purpose, you first have to be willing to make the journey. It may be a long and one, it may require a lot of trial and error, but everything worthwhile does.

Find your purpose

When you have a purpose, you know that you're a part of something much bigger than yourself and your surroundings. It means that you're needed, that you're making a valuable contribution, and that you're enriching the lives of those around you. It's what prepares you for what's ahead. The 'why' matters, because when you know why you're doing what you're doing, you have something to look forward to. Finding your purpose is the first step towards achieving your goals. So eventually, you can help create a sense of purpose for others as well. The most fulfilled and successful people don't just work towards succeeding and thriving in their careers. They also strive to improve the lives of others. Below are 4 essential steps to help you find your purpose for a more meaningful life.

Take action

Overthinking and constantly weighing your options won't help you get anywhere. If anything, you'll be running around in circles or tracing your steps back to where it all went wrong. Instead of dithering or getting flustered, choose to take action. Not to toot my own horn, though it may sound that way, this is probably the one thing I can congruently say I excel at. I do extensive research, I do some planning, and I make sure to cover all the bases. However, what I don't do is ponder too much. I know a lot of people that talk themselves out of starting something or taking action. I also know that there will always be a hundred reasons not to do something. After all, nothing is certain, except death! So, if you get excited by something, I urge you to try it out, even if others tell you not to. Give it a go, if it works, then that's splendid, and if it doesn't then fine! Learn from it and move on. You can always take a calculated risk, what you can't do is reverse or overturn your regrets. Stop daydreaming about the perfect life and start taking steps towards your goals. This will get you out of your head so you learn what works and what doesn't, as well as what's truly important to you and what doesn't matter. The sooner you start taking action, the sooner you get to see the results.

Trust your instinct

Have you ever stopped to listen to what you consider to be the pesky voice inside your head? Maybe it keeps telling you "This is what I truly want to do." No matter how scary of a leap it might be, sometimes, you just have to trust your instinct. Don't be afraid of that voice, don't shut it out. Let it motivate you so you can push yourself to explore unexpected opportunities and options.

Put yourself under scrutiny

What are your passions, your hobbies, the things that you cannot wait to get to once you're done with your daily chores and tasks? What inspires you the most? Take the time to observe yourself from the outside and see what you can identify. Then look into how you can tie your passion with your purpose. Perhaps one can nurture the other or give you a strong burst of motivation to work harder to achieve your goals.

The sooner you understand what it is that drives you, the sooner you can organize your life to propel you into the job of your dreams, or push you to become a business owner and when you pour your heart and soul into that one thing you were made for; you can use it to inspire others around you as well.

The Spiritual

The spiritual aspect of your existence is your connection to your essence; it represents self-love, self-respect, and self-compassion, but also spiritual guidance. For some, it could be more interlaced with religion than spirituality. For others, it could have more to do with the quantum energy that all living organisms are made of. While I am not religious, I do understand the value that religion brings to many people's lives. For me personally, my sense of spirituality both stems from and is aimed towards self-love and happiness.

Accessing the spiritual aspect of our being is essential to re-establish balance in our lives. When we're living in misalignment with our values, this dissonance translates into our state of being which leads us to feel unhappy, unfulfilled and out of place.

Self-acceptance is the first step to take if you want to improve your spiritual well-being. Your "one year to live" plan shouldn't focus on the things you cannot change, the things beyond your control, or the things that cannot be mended. It should rather put emphasis on what you can do and all the ways in which you can evolve.

This is why a daily spiritual or religious practice is so important to stay grounded and direct your attention toward what matters the most. To reach a state of utter harmony between each of the layers of your existence, you need to develop your intuition just as much as you do your mind, emotions, and physical body to create a solid foundation.

Practices for Spiritual Wellness

Start your day with gratitude:

People often forget just how critical a gratitude mindset is. Instead of viewing everything as a major inconvenience or a setback, being appreciative and grateful allows you to find the silver lining in every situation. Ultimately, you won't view challenges as obstacles but rather as opportunities to learn from and grow.

When you start your day either by listing five things you're grateful for or by enjoying the power of the present moment, you're better equipped to deal with difficulties as they arise. You also learn to be more mindful of your surroundings. Usually, it's just a matter of deciding to be grateful, and when you do, you get to experience immense fulfilment from developing this habit and all the good it fosters.

End your day by writing down one thing you are thankful for:

"It's not about having what you want, but wanting what you have." This goes hand in hand with starting your day by practicing gratitude. We often feel unsatisfied with what we have. This is brought about by not realizing just how valuable and important the things in our possession already are. So, if you make it a habit to write down one thing you're thankful for at the end of each day, it can serve as an uplifting reminder of all the important things you already have.

Chapter Five:

Time for Action

While we might enjoy cradling the ethereal sensation of ideas, plans, and thoughts, one must come to understand that plans only come to fruition if they are materialized by action. One of the more interesting facts about us is that we become more motivated and unyielding of our ideals and goals the more we do things. Action is everything, in fact, it is the fruit-bearing tree of our goals.

Often in life, people become more motivated by action when it has a deadline for becoming in the real world. While you had time to think over your plans on what to do after you've been made aware of your predicament, one thing should come to mind and that is the fact that you've had your whole life to think things over. Though one year to live can't grant you enough time to become an astronaut, it can be enough to create change within you and the world around you now and in the future.

The eternal in all of us

In one of the greatest publications ever made, Marcus Aurelius notes down his life in a book called: "To himself." This book now has become one of the best sellers in the entire world under the name: Mediations. This book was never meant to be published to the world, in fact, Marcus Aurelius, a Stoic Roman Emperor, wrote this book to himself only. It is now regarded as one of the most insightful in regard to one's death.

"It is not death that a man should fear, but rather he should fear never beginning to live."

—Marcus Aurelius

Marcus Aurelius also notes down that death is not the end of someone's being, but it is only the resolution of their physical other half, a transitory phase where the physical matter blends with the immaterial becoming a part of the universe. While aware that one's existence will cease to be, Marcus is also aware that one's actions can and will immortalize us. Our body is a mere manifestation, a materialization of what our DNA is, and it is the other half of the twin that is us. Matter and energy are the basis on which we understand the world, they are neither the same nor contradictory, however, they do complement each other. Whether you're a spiritual person or not, you must realize that there is something real behind energy. As tough as a block of steel might look, it's merely atoms bound together by energy.

All things considered, one must realize that the twin half of our being, matter, can only be accessed by action. In other words, the action is the culmination of our goal, but not the goal itself. Action is what decides the fate of our existence, whether our actions get to tell our story once our body has decayed is all up to us and what we DO.

What is the action?

In short, action is doing what we plan on doing. To act is to materialize your thoughts into the tangible. In other words, action is the process by which energy becomes matter. There is a point to the cliché: Action speaks louder than words. While most people misinterpret what it means, action is merely voicing your words and thoughts. It's translating your thoughts into things. Action is also what vocalizes your goals and makes them real.

In the previous chapter that spoke about planning, it should be clear at this point that this section about planning is twofold. The first part about action should be about living the rest of your life to the fullest, and the second is about living past your life. While your body, the physical, will decay, your actions can keep you going. It's not that we should seek to be immortals. In fact, we should seek to find a conclusion of ourselves, one that we're content with.

Action about living the rest of your life

While applying what was said and mentioned in chapter four, you should just move on and materialize it in this phase. Not everyone's bucket list is going to consist of those earth-shattering action-packed activities like skydiving. Your goal on the bucket list is to do the things YOU have always wanted, not what other people made you think is always cool. With that piece of paper, you wrote, look at the goals you've envisioned very carefully and think not just when you will do them, but also how. It should also be evident that now is the time to do them because hesitation is not an option.

You might not realize it yet, but congratulations! You've already done the first step when it comes to action and that is when you wrote your goals and aspirations down. There is something real and tangible about writing your goals down, it makes them come to life. At last, you've gone out of your head and made an action and that is writing this down.

Action about going past your life

Your actions decide not only the fate of your life from now to the point where your body will decay -morbid of me to say, I know, but also your overall story, and the rest of the world. The actions that Tesla, Ford, Andrew Carnegie, and Abraham Lincoln have taken are all ones that might not have made much change in their era, but they have certainly decided the fate of the world for decades and even centuries. Though they're now long dead, their actions are still with us. Likewise, regardless of your status or ability, the actions you take will decide the story that is told about you and how the world will change. Every book you've read, every music you've tuned in to, and every meal you've had are all still with you and will always be.

Whether the actions you take for the past life are in order to help someone or help the world, they WILL create change. You might decide to help your family, support projects and things you stand for, or just leave your words for the world to read, they will create something that changes people. For better or worse, every action we've taken has changed the world in some way or another. For all we know, it is actions that we take that create metamorphosis which is necessary for life. Even our body is in a continuous cycle of metamorphosis. Every atom of our body changes as we grow older, but our actions remain forever.

Why is action so important?

Habit is the exercise for action, the more we do something, the better we get at it. This does not just apply to the application of habits, such as waking up early or doing work, but it is also in the instance of taking action. The more we take action, the easier it gets to take action.

The law of diminishing intent is something you've most certainly experienced in life. We intend to do something in the heat of the moment, we romanticize something on New Year's Eve, think about our goals and how exciting they all are, but we never really act on them. It happens to the best of us.

While we must never act on impulses, make decisions when we're angry, or make promises when we're optimistic and hopeful, our thoughts and ideas never become real unless we make them real. The more we sit on the idea, the vaguer our motivation for it seems. The motivation we've all had to lose those dozens of pounds on the first of January at 1 am seems a bit more abstract and unrealistic on the morning of January 2nd. This feeds into the cycle of days until we completely forget about what we intend on doing. While emotions can certainly blind us into doing the wrong things, our logical self is sometimes, to put it bluntly, a coward. We must use those emotions and that fire to fuel the spark of the first step. Taking action is all that needs to be done, but the first step is all that matters.

Discipline is capturing and immortalizing emotion and transforming it into equity. Therefore, we must value that emotion, understand it, and let it fuel our actions. These are some of the reasons why taking action is so important when you've accomplished the first step which is to note down your goals.

In addition to that, one must also understand the process by which action is taken. To this, we must go back and think about the effects that action has on us. Everything we do affects everything else and it all starts with the first action. If we don't take the smallest step to start, we will never do the big one at the end. Now here is the good news: it all starts with the smallest step.

Another piece of good news is that the more we do those small steps, the more we are willing to take the big challenge and before you know it, the hardest bullet point on your bucket list seems so realistic that you can feel it already. The importance of taking action lies in your self-worth. The bad news is that the smallest setback can also erode your psyche. The more we 'ease up', the less likely we are to push through and finish what we started. The way these small setbacks gnaw at our self-confidence is evident in how we follow through with our actions. One instance of lack of action leads to another. While we might think to ourselves that it is only one small action that has no change in the real world, the truth is that it does have a change and it is on us.

The same as the way a page leads to another, that massive book that seemed gargantuan is now simply pages. Step by step, your actions can be materialized if you follow the rule of the smallest discipline. After a certain point, it will become harder to stop your actions than it is to continue, much like once you're thirty pages deep in a one thousand-page book. The law of diminishing intent becomes the sunk cost effect.

The Wheel of Life action guide

Something as abstract as taking action might seem monumental which is why categorizing action to be taken in the 365 days or so you have left is extremely vital. The wheel of life is something you ought to always have in mind, especially in action.

Mental action

In the mental side of action, there are two gateways: contribution and growth. They both feed into each other. Growth as an individual is an important part of life especially as we mature. Fundamentally, mental growth action-taking is very important as it sets how your story will conclude. Likewise, it's just as important to purify your mind of wicked ideas as it is to fill it with healthy productive ones. Here are ways to add value growth when it comes to the mental:

Mindfulness: Becoming more mindful of everything around your life is key. It boils down to appreciating the little things in life. Being mindful of things around your life such as your health, relationships, the food you eat and the people you surround yourself with can add a lot of colour to your life.

Understanding: understanding the world and the universe is also something that can really energize your mental side. Understanding starts with mindfulness and knowing. So, knowing more is always something you should strive at. Seek to learn a few things each day that mean something to you. Make it a habit to research, know more, and come to conclusions every time your mind begins to wander about.

Actions to take

- Limit your social media exposure -I realize how hard this can be, especially considering how ubiquitous social media is in this day and age, but like all things, balance is key. What you consume might bring you temporary relief, a short-lived sense of enjoyment or pleasure, but you have to consider the question: "Does this serve me and my goals in the long term?" I agree, not everything has to have a purpose, and some idleness won't necessarily kill you, but social media can easily end up consuming you if you don't balance it out with some valuable content.

- Read knowledge and books you absolutely enjoy
- Write and journal about your days
- Always stay positive, no matter what
- Steer clear from unnecessary conflict -conflict is mandatory sometimes. It's especially worthwhile when the outcome helps you become better or improve some area of your life.
- Always be in the moment, neither in the past nor future -while this doesn't entail not thinking about the future at all or not reminiscing over the past, as these encounters can often be a source of motivation or inspiration, you also need to ensure you're enjoying the present to make the most out of its precious moments.

Physical action

We might think of ourselves as energy floating in the air, but at the end of the day our body, the physical twin half, is still what carries and embodies that energy. We're still made from flesh and bones. Our physical health can greatly influence our mental, spiritual, and emotional side for it is the material. While you might think that taking care of your health at this point is futile since you only have a year to live, you'd be very wrong. If you plan on living the rest of your life, the year left to live to the fullest, then you ought to take care of that vessel as much as you can because the health of your physical body is almost synonymous with the health of your mental, emotional, and spiritual side. Here are ways you can do this:

One year to live

Lifestyle changes: You don't need to be an athlete in a family of Olympic medallists to live a healthy life. In fact, it all starts with your lifestyle habits. Taking a walk every day, being as active as you can, and being aware of the nutrition you put into your body are vital. The saying: "You are what you eat" is very real, in fact, it is literally what it says, and you are what you eat. You become what you eat, in fact. Even the amino acids you digest from the protein you eat become the building block of the tissue inside your body which in turn gives you the energy to take action. So be mindful and aware of the foods you eat -for the most part, you should strive to enjoy yourself every now and then, as long as it's in moderation.

Stability: None of us need billions of dollars to live a happy life, but let's not kid ourselves, money is very important when it comes to happiness. Literal paper money might not give you happiness, but the things it provides can indeed make you happy. For instance, while you might not be happy with the money you have, other people might be. That said, money is important to ensure that you have a roof over your head, a warm bed, clean clothes, and a hearty meal. Things we might take for granted, but they are very important for the physical side. Not everyone's financial situation is the same, but ensuring you have enough finances is critical.

Actions to take

- Walk at least forty minutes every day
- Stay active as much as you can
- Be balanced in your exercise routine

- Follow your doctor's orders but be open to alternative opinions -not all doctors know everything!
- Take care of your body with proper hygiene and maintenance
- Don't be afraid of changing your wardrobe into something you enjoy having on
- Continue working if needed in order to provide for yourself, or others
- Seize every moment you live

Emotional action

We are and have always been social beings, the reason why we're the apex of the earth is because of our relationships. Because we helped each other with what we could and relied on others for what they can do for us, we grew stronger. Nothing has changed in the last two hundred thousand years, we're still the social beings we were back when we were hunter-gatherers and our relationships quite literally define us. This is why we are so keen on what people think of us. In fact, one of the greatest fears about death is not the fear of not existing, it's the fear of what people may think of us after we die.

Bronnie Ware, the author of "The Top Five Regrets of the Dying" has spent a large part of her life with patients who had less than three months to live. Her memoir is interesting because she spent time with people who were on their deathbed most of the time caring for them. Their top regrets had absolutely nothing to do with work, money, status, power or any of that. In fact, this was universal in all of them. Some of those patients were an extremely rich, and some were barely scraping by, but their biggest regrets all had to do with the lack of spending time with those they loved the most.

It's very interesting how some of the most business-minded people that devote their whole life to a goal almost always end up regretting how they did not spend enough time with their loved ones.

Cherish those you love: It's almost always the case that when people die, others only remember the good things about them. Just think to yourself about someone who died in your life, you will almost always think about the good memories you've had with them, and rarely the moments that upset you. Therefore, make it a conscious effort, a habit almost, to look after the people you love the most and spend quality time with them.

Live your relationships to the fullest

Our romantic relationships are often one of the biggest pillars of our life. In fact, a huge driving force we all have is to find the right mate and live our lives to the fullest with them. It is for that reason that your romantic relationship with your significant other must be fulfilling. Now is definitely not the time to engage in squanders. Think about this from their perspective, when you eventually pass away, they will be left alone by themselves for a long time. Though grief and melancholy might take over for some days, what's important is that they reminisce about the times you've spent. More likely than not, these are going to be the last days you spend with them.

Actions to take

- Never skip family gatherings
- Spend time with your family
- Make amends
- Literally, tell the people you love how much you do
- Show the people you love how much you love them
- Value your relationship with your significant other
- Plan as many experiences with your significant other as time would allow
- Forgive others you've clashed with

Spiritual action

People mystify the mystical far too often to the point of illusion. The spiritual does not have to be too dreamy or unworldly, in fact, it is right there with you. It's generally easier to rejuvenate and salve the relationships you have with others, even your enemies. Nevertheless, our relationship with the self is the most complex of all. We hold the burden of not forgiving which prevents us from loving ourselves. If you're now in the labyrinth of self-hate which starts with hating yourself and continues on to hating yourself for doing the latter, you'll find that you're in the cycle that feeds on itself, like an immortal ouroboros (ancient symbol depicting a serpent or dragon eating its own tail.). This has to stop.

Meditation

Seemingly inactive, mediation might seem like an activity that amounts to nothing. However, this notion is highly erroneous. Meditation is letting go of your ego, the babbling monkey inside every one of your heads. Meditation also allows us to access what's further deep and special about us. It's letting go of all one's fears, succumbing to all imaginations, and accessing our higher self, the spiritual. Arrange a time every day, maybe multiple times per day, to access the higher self. I strongly believe that you can meditate anywhere, anytime -no offense to hardcore meditation gurus. I am still an advocate of this practice; I just have my own style and so should you.

- This isn't about gods, angels, or ghosts, it's about you. Personally, I like to go for a meditative walk early in the morning and that's what I consider to be my form of meditation. Spend time meditating daily.
- Read or listen to the works of philosophers you connect with the most
- Keep a gratitude journal
- Listen to your instincts more
- Let go of envy

The wheel of life resembles a four-way gear, simultaneously turning with each tooth of gear segueing into more action eventually transmitting motion. However, if one gear is decayed or corrupt, the gears will grind and there won't be any motion. In fact, one rusted gear can snowball into all of the gears breaking down at some point. Understanding this is pivotal to taking action in your life.

Do you want to know who you are? Don't ask. Act! Action will delineate and define you.

- Thomas Jefferson

The action plan for taking action

While most of us can come up with a list of 100 things we want to do in the midst of euphoria, it's important to be more methodical about the action we take. After all, preparation is half the battle already won.

Step 1: Write each goal in your to-do list on a separate paper or section

Start by looking at the overall list and then write each and every one of those goals in a separate paper or section. This is going to help you to break down that huge wall into boulders and then into small steps.

Step 2: Under each goal, write every step you can take right now or as soon as possible

The law of diminishing intent is absolutely no joke, we can seriously lose interest in the things we plan on doing simply by doing them. Therefore, you should try to take the first step in each of the goals you've created as fast as possible. Whether this is asking your boss for a raise you deserve, or planting trees, start now, send that email for a meeting or buy the shovel for that oak tree. It's now or never!

Step 3: Hold yourself accountable for everything you've set out to do

There is no one but yourself who is going to be held accountable, you're the creator of your destiny and the writer of your story, so be the guardian of your fate and don't buckle.

Step 4: Start with the smallest and easiest goal

A common mistake people often make is thinking that they should start with the hardest and most difficult task. This could not be farther from the truth. Unless the goal you strive for is time-related and the sooner you start it the better, there is no reason why you should not work on the smallest and easiest goal on your list. This feeds into the next goal and by the time you're head-on with the hardest goal, you cannot quit on it because you've already achieved all of the other goals, so what's another?

There is no perfect time

One of modern life's worst misconceptions is that there is a perfect time for everything. There is a time for everything, but a perfect time is not one of them. You, more than anyone, should be the wisest to know that there is no perfect time for anything at all. I started my own business, an MMA gym during the Covid-19 lockdown and while many would have deemed this to be an unsound decision to make, I am glad I followed through with it. Most people had shut down their gyms, some even went bankrupt. But I knew the situation was

Time for Action

bound to get better and even if it didn't, I could at least say I went for it and did my best to make it happen. If I waited, if I pondered too much, I might have had more competition, and I might have just decided not to do it altogether.

A great tragedy is that most people take their ideas with them to the graveyard. They wait for the right moment and the right time, but time ceases to exist and that idea never comes to fruition. In fact, even you who might be reading this might think that you have one year to live and that you will surely have a year to live, but nothing in life is certain.

One of the greatest sayings about doing something right now and not later or tomorrow is from Les Brown:

"The graveyard is the richest place on earth because it is here that you will find all the hopes and dreams that were never fulfilled, the books that were never written, the songs that were never sung, the inventions that were never shared, the cures that were never discovered, all because someone was too afraid to take that first step, keep with the problem, or determined to carry out their dream." -Les Brown

Death is an event no one in the world can escape, don't think that other people in the world who are walking around, little children, young couples full of love, or entrepreneurs planning their next million-dollar project are more blessed than you are. Everyone has an end time to which they cease to exist no matter how much money they have or what they did in the world. However, when you die, you must leave no goal behind.

Taking action is everything that matters in the world and everything that stands between you and taking action is simply the first step. Dreams can come true, but dreams require action after you transmute your desire into a goal that is backed by a plan. After all, talk is cheap, so do you have what it takes to take action right now?

> *"The impediment to action advances action. What stands in the way becomes the way."*
>
> Marcus Aurelius- "Meditations"

Chapter Six :

Reflection and Measure

While pursuing personal growth and development, you don't always take measures to track your progress, especially considering how elusive and unquantifiable some of the aspects you're working to improve can be. So, it can be difficult to determine where you're at. This chapter is designed to help you measure your personal growth. You will find a number of steps, tools, and methods that you can use to facilitate the process of evaluating your life and keeping track of your goals.

Your definition of success concerning personal growth won't necessarily be the same for someone else. With that said, succeeding often entails more than simply achieving a particular set of goals. When you put in the effort and invest in yourself, you should see results in many areas of your life. Measuring those results begins with practicing self-awareness, studying the trends, assessing progress, evaluating your technique, and adjusting your timeline.

Practice self-awareness

To measure your personal growth, you first need to cultivate some degree of self-awareness. This is what helps you stay grounded in the reality of the present moment. When you practice self-awareness, you're less likely to minimize or overstate the truth about your progress and your abilities.

Practicing self-awareness entails a level of honesty and vulnerability that not everyone is open to. If you lack this self-consciousness and awareness, then it becomes almost impossible to identify where you're currently at and get a tangible idea of your progress. Not only that but you're essentially oblivious to your personal growth and development.

You simply cannot afford to only gauge the superficial things in your life and how they're going. You have to be prepared to go deeper and examine what lies beneath the surface, i.e. your emotions and thoughts. Being aware of your reality as others see it is easy, but being aware of unconscious habits, behaviours, and emotions that you don't put much thought into is the real challenge.

Uncovering those patterns of thought that govern your perception and the way you act or react is key to making a lasting change. Introspection is vital when it comes to implementing better habits that will push you to accomplish your goals within the time frame you have set for yourself.

Reflection should occur inwards first before you move on to gauging external factors and circumstances. This isn't always easy, especially if you're used to filling all the silences with noise, but sitting with yourself and prompting a comfortable and truthful environment where you can be as honest as possible is fundamental to ensuring a positive outcome and sustaining your progress.

Study the trends

Following your one-year to live plan means you will be better at the end of that year than you were the day you started. And while that statement can be true, based on how much work and effort you put in, it still doesn't mean that that progress will follow the same curve, and so it doesn't necessarily mean that you'll be better in the year to come.

While looking back to your past is generally a good way to see how far you've come, it shouldn't be the only tool you use to measure your personal growth. Looking at your past personal growth can be insightful, but, alone, it can also be outdated. This is why it's important to track your progress both as you go and in the near past.

Sure, your life might be better now than it was a year ago, but it also might have been significantly better four months ago than now. Studying the trends as they occur is paramount because it provides you with a highly effective tool for measuring your progress.

So, ask yourself- how is my month going? Is it better than last month? How is my week, my day? You won't always be doing well, and you shouldn't expect yourself to be because that introduces a variety of impossible standards to maintain, and that will only sabotage your progress in the long run.

In fact, dips and low points are completely normal and should be anticipated. However, it's important to be aware of those dips and catch on to them as soon as possible. Your lows can be very telling, they provide you with data that shows what you're doing wrong and so, in turn, they can point you in the right direction. Paying attention to how your progress unfolds can also highlight signs of stagnation when you feel that nothing is changing. Realizing this helps you consider new methods and approaches to induce some growth.

Assess progress

Assessing your progress is not just a step you should aim to take at the end of each month or by the end of the year. This is an inherent part of the process and so it should be an important component of your daily routine. The main thing that tends to turn people away from the ability to assess their goals and accomplish what they hoped for is the feeling of being stuck and not getting anywhere.

You need to be upfront with yourself during each assessment or evaluation. Which goals have you made progress on, and which goals are you struggling with? You can't possibly determine how much farther you have to go without measuring your progress, just like you can't determine what adjustments you need to make to achieve your goals.

In most cases, measuring entails units, numbers, and percentages. If your goal, for instance, is to pay back your debts, then your progress comes down to how much you have paid thus far and how much you have left. A more detailed account would include a record of the months you were able to pay more or less and why.

Examining your bank statements in accordance with your personal calendar would allow you to identify the special occasions on which you had to spend some extra money. This assessment will help you analyse the recurring expenses that prevent you from paying the debt back either more quickly or more consistently. Keeping track of what you're achieving along the way will inform your progress and help you reach your goals.

Evaluate your technique

You can't assess your progress without evaluating your approach and how it affects the process. This is why you have to invest some time in examining the techniques, tools, and methods that you're relying on to accomplish your goals. Not every plan you map out will go exactly as you imagined it to unfold and not every technique will yield the positive outcomes you expected. What you do and how you proceed is just as important as the end result you aim to achieve.

- Are you completing tasks in a timely manner?
- Is there something in your approach that you could change or alter?
- Is there something else you might want to consider?

- Are there any particular concerns that you believe are holding you back?
- Is there any way you can overcome those in an efficient way?
- Should you adjust your goal in some way?

Once you take these questions into account, you can determine the areas in which you are succeeding as well as those in which you are struggling. This, in turn, will help you better understand what is pushing you to succeed and what is standing in your way or holding you back from accomplishing your goals.

You will find that planning ahead of time and anticipating drawbacks will leave you feeling much more prepared and much less blindsided by surprising events or unexpected outcomes. Subsequently, being prepared will help you complete the tasks and meet the goals you've set for yourself a lot more consistently. The important step here is to continue making assessments of what works and why, to determine how you can apply this to the other aspects of your life as well.

Don't be quick to dismiss what doesn't work or push it to the side as soon as you realize it's hindering your progress because there's tremendous value in asking why your efforts failed and why your approach didn't bring the results you wanted.

For example, if your goal is to push yourself out of your comfort zone this year by doing more of the things that scare you and so far, you've only done five out of your list of hundred, why do you think that is? Does your daily routine not allow you to complete some of the items on your "one year to live bucket list?" Are some of those items too out there for you to try so soon? Do you not feel confident enough to carry out those goals?

Look at your daily routine, the nature of the goals you've set, and the skills these require then get to the bottom of it. Evaluate all the factors that come into play and examine the situations in which you succeed and in which you struggle, then try to recreate the circumstances where you usually are more prone to reach your desired outcome.

Taking the time to assess what you're doing and how you're doing it will help you understand what works in terms of completing tasks, and therefore help you realize better ways to meet your goals.

Adjust your timeline

Once you determine your progress, it's time to adjust your timeline accordingly. There is nothing wrong with being ambitious when goal setting, in fact, it's encouraged. With that said, in the midst of the excitement a new plan invokes, sometimes you can be too ambitious, which means, you will most likely overestimate the number of things you can get done within a set time frame.

When that occurs, don't be unkind to yourself or feel too bad for not being able to accomplish everything in time. You will most likely need to rethink your overall deadline for those big long-term goals, and you might even have to change them up as you reach each milestone. Incremental assessments of your goals are essential, and you should expect to adjust your timeline accordingly. When you do this, you allow yourself more room to learn from each milestone and apply those learnings going forward.

How to track your progress

Growth and development are not always the easiest to measure, especially considering how personal of an experience these tend to be. Your idea of success may not necessarily be your father's idea of success, and vice versa. So, what they may consider a great result, you might view as insignificant or futile. This is why tracking your progress in terms of personal growth can be challenging. With that said, there are some tools that can make this process easier for your mind to absorb and grasp.

- **Journaling**

Keeping a journal or some other form of documentation is a great way to record and track your thoughts, feelings, and emotions, but also your successes, failures, and goal progress. This pushes you to make reflection part of your daily routine. Not only that but having your experiences written down on paper also helps you examine the challenging aspects of working toward your goals.

The mind is a very complex and multi-layered machine. And unless you're a very organized person, it's going to be extremely difficult to catch up with. There's so much going on at all times that you expend the majority of your mental energy trying to keep up with your mind's activity.

Taking the time to capture that information and document it will help you process it better. Some of the thoughts you write down won't necessarily serve you or inform your progress, so you will have to let them go. Others can provide you with invaluable insights into the elements that are helping you progress and those that are obstructing your way.

By keeping a journal, you bring those catalysts and challenges out of the deep end of your mind and into your conscious awareness. Journaling does not always have to follow a specific template or answer a particular set of prompts. Setting aside as little as ten minutes out of your entire day for journaling can help remind you of how far you've come and keep track of your victories, no matter how small. You might be surprised a year from now when you look back on this day and remember it as the first step of a life-changing journey.

- **Habit tracking apps**

Some say it takes twenty-one days to form a habit, others say it takes sixty-six days. Regardless of how long the process of habit-forming can be, beginning and maintaining a better routine is challenging. It requires tremendous determination, willpower, and discipline. It's a process that you need to stay on top of at all times.

Perseverance is key, but so is having an incentive that encourages you to stay on track. Habit tracker apps can help keep you accountable for the goals you set for yourself. These apps tend to be a great alternative to journaling because they're more structured and forward than the subjective experience of keeping a journal and documenting your thoughts and emotions at a given moment.

One year to live

Your one-year to live plan will probably include a number of big goals and milestones. Long-term goals can be overwhelming especially because of the series of steps and commitments they entail. These will often be intimidating -so intimidating that it might deter you from starting in the first place.

Using a habit tracker can give you small victories to look forward to on a daily basis. It also allows you to see the progress you're making in real time, which in itself is a great source of motivation and a confidence booster.

- **Planners and detailed schedules**

While I am not doubting your cognitive abilities when it comes to tracking all the professional and personal demands you're subject to, I do believe that using daily, weekly, and monthly planners can make your life a lot easier. Not only does a thorough schedule and a detailed planner take the stress out of planning important tasks but it also improves your productivity and helps you maintain an effective schedule.

Having one somewhere accessible like your wall or desktop can facilitate goal and progress tracking. That way you can see how your day/week/month is going without feeling lost and overwhelmed by the endless list of tasks you have to complete within the deadline you set for yourself.

Planners and schedules can also be a more practical alternative to journaling because they're so great for tracking habits, planning goals, and staying up to date with the progress you're making in the different areas of your life.

There are many things you can track in relation to your personal growth, including but not limited to successes, failures, thoughts, actions, moods, emotions, feelings, confidence, self-esteem, goals, habits, and even how you spend your time.

Alternative ways to assess your progress

Goals that have definite endpoints are easier to track because you know when you've accomplished them. On the other hand, long-term goals take time, and by extension, they require a series of steps and tasks that will occupy most of your time. You might be making progress on one front but not so much on the others, which can be hard to track.

This is why defining your success should involve both long-term goals and the actions you take every day. In addition to that, you also need to maintain a certain balance that will allow you to carry out your "one year to live plan" as intended. Because this can be daunting, it may be more helpful to consider alternative tools for evaluating yourself as you go.

Define what success means for you on a daily basis

At the start of each day, take a moment to reflect and meditate on how you'd like your day to unfold. Learning how to prioritize is an important skill that can help you accomplish more while doing less.

Making significant progress in every conceivable area of your life is great, but it probably won't happen quickly. So, you have to be realistic about what you want to achieve and determine what is most important to you at that moment. This will allow you to stay focused as you work on bringing your definition of success to life.

Create new metrics

We often use metrics in our professional goals, and while they do facilitate goal and progress tracking, they're not a universal unit of measurement. As I have mentioned before, personal growth is not something palpable that you can easily compute or estimate.

Making an assessment of how much you can save on a monthly basis is not the same as making a projection of how much you can grow as a person. The metrics you use to determine the former won't be appropriate to evaluate the latter.

So, for example, if you're seeking more harmony in your life, better spiritual alignment, or healthier and more meaningful relationships, you will need a different way to quantify those goals and stay on track with that particular aspect of your life, which, in turn, necessitates creating some new metrics.

For instance, if you're looking to create a new habit like keeping in touch with your friends or spending more quality time with your family, you should phrase that goal in a way that facilitates making an assessment further down the line.

Something along the lines of "I will call/text one of my friends every day", "I will spend forty minutes of undisturbed and distraction-free time with my family every day." These goals relate to an easy metric, which is the number of days you practiced this habit.

Answer three questions on a daily basis

If you find progress tracking to be somewhat elusive, you can take a different approach and ask yourself these three questions at the end of the day:

- How am I feeling?
- Did I do what I wanted to do? And, how much of it?
- Did today matter?

You could spend some time reflecting on your to-do list and reviewing your planner. But when you ask yourself these questions, you will probably know the answer intuitively. If today mattered, then great, follow that pattern tomorrow.

If you can't think of anything that made a difference, then change things up and try a different approach.

Take the time to write down your answers to these three questions, even if it's just a sentence or two. Then throughout the following day, reflect on those answers whenever you get a chance to choose how you spend your time.

Remember that although measuring your progress and personal growth is an important part of the process, it's normal to encounter low points and go through failures. You have to embrace the downs just as you would embrace the ups.

Accept them for what they are and turn them into an opportunity for more growth and learning. There's no need to beat yourself up. Making mistakes is an inherent part of the journey and it can be a moment of invaluable reflection that helps you grow stronger and wiser.

Part 2
Possible Roadblocks

Chapter Seven:

How to Change Your State

"Any person capable of angering you becomes your master."

- Epictetus

**The following chapters (7 to 10) are centred around you developing the right mindset to follow through with your one-year to life plan. They are based on changing your state, your focus, your discipline, and your habits.

A mother rescues her daughter from fire and perishes, a father saves his children from a riptide and meets his and demise, parents push their daughter out of a sinking car and drown ... There are countless stories and endless accounts describing heroic acts of mothers and fathers in their last attempts to ensure their children's survival. As tragic as these stories are, they also represent a rendition of how deep and complex human emotion is. A desperate decision made in a moment of crisis can define a family's legacy. There is no shadow of a doubt that these instances of parental sacrifice have been re-enacted countless times throughout history.

Evolutionary biologists explain these sacrifices in terms of reproductive success, ensuring the passing of one's genes to future generations. With that said, we simply cannot reduce these decisions to our mere human instincts. This exemplary act is an insight into the potency of our emotions. It suggests that our feelings, longings, and passions are fundamental guides that we owe not just to our survival but our entire existence. The urgency this situation presents, that of rescuing one's beloved child is so powerful it overrides the proclivity of survival.

This choice may not be rational when objectively looked at and dissected, but viewing it under a different light, that of the extraordinary hold of emotions, we understand that it wasn't only the best decision to make but also the only one. This dominance of emotions over logic in such critical instances is why emotions occupy a central role in the psyche. They're our guiding light when we're faced with predicaments that are far too detrimental to leave to logic alone.

Danger, pain, loss, suffering, grief, joy, happiness, longing ... Each one of these emotions equips you with a readiness to act, it pushes you to handle the challenges you're facing, to persist in your efforts toward achieving a goal, or to simply stop and appreciate the present moment. It's the voice that tells you what to do when no guidebook or person will. You've never been much aware of it, it never explicitly substantializes until you genuinely need it. It's imprinted in your neurons, an innate predilection of the metaphoric human heart.

If we are to truly comprehend human nature, neglecting to examine the power of emotions is certainly imprudent. We've come to place so much emphasis on the importance and the value of what is purely rational that we've disregarded how our emotional intelligence shapes our actions and decisions. And although our emotions have proven much wisdom in their guidance, the realities of modern society established themselves to be deeply anchored in matters of ethics and reason. So much so that we've begun to resent our emotions, deeming them frivolous, unstable, and subject to volatility.

But if we analyse the etymology of the word 'emotion' we find that it comes from the Latin verb *motere*, which means 'to move.' This suggests that our emotions are rooted in our impulses to take action. The tendency to 'do something' is implicit no matter what emotion we might be dealing with. Sometimes, what we choose to do in a given situation might not be the ideal course of action. The emotions we feel can be so strong, so deafening, that we fail to see the current reality for what it is.

For instance, a father shoots his 14-year-old son thinking he was an intruder. The example provided, while drastic, offers us an insight into how much of an impact our emotional state can have on our thoughts, feelings, and actions. It proves the extent these emotions have on our survival as well as our undoing. Emotions are complex, they can be confusing and are often misunderstood.

How to Change Your State

We're constantly told that we need to get our emotions in check because they can cloud our judgment and prevent us from accomplishing our goals. We see our emotions as a weakness, as an entity to be conquered. They're disruptive, they can wreak havoc on our world, and they can cause acute embarrassment, sorrowful regret, and so much unnecessary suffering. But emotions are a mere response to the stimulus we experience from our surroundings.

Sometimes negative emotions stem from discomfort, hardships, and failures, while other times they're the result of toxic beliefs, negative perspectives, and impossible expectations. While we need that innate pilot to guide us through our daily lives, when it starts to take over, influence other aspects of our existence, and impede our ability to take action, that's a warning sign that requires our immediate attention.

It means there is something to be addressed or remedied, whether it be changing the environment we're in, or shifting our beliefs and our responses to that environment. This is crucial because your emotions can extend themselves to your physiology and even your focus. When you're sad or depressed, those negative emotions translate themselves into how you sit and the way you present yourself. You slump and slouch, you sit, stand, and walk as discreetly as you can, your body is trying to make itself small, to occupy as little space as possible, it's afraid of its own weight.

Your brain associates the negative emotions you are feeling with your stance, and then that stance becomes a habit, and the negative emotions persist. When you're in that emotional state, all you can detect and focus on in your surroundings is but a confirmation of your emotions and what you're feeling in that moment. You wake up feeling funky, you're in a bad mood, and the last thing you want is to have your patience tested at work. Of course, the coffee machine happens to break down that day. Of course, all of your presentable shirts happen to be dirty. Of course, you happen to get a flat tire before even leaving the house. Of course, some jerk happens to randomly cut you off at the highway exit. These are the things you notice that further amplify those negative emotions.

But you didn't notice that your favourite song was playing on the radio, you didn't notice that the weather was nice that morning, you didn't notice that the plant you've been watering for weeks has begun to bloom, you didn't notice that sweet text your friend sent you. So many things are left unappreciated, gone unnoticed, simply because you gave in to your emotions and you let them override the simple act of being.

Having one year to live certainly puts things in perspective. It triggers all kinds of emotions. Fear of dying perhaps, fear of not having enough time to accomplish everything you want to accomplish, fear of saying goodbye to friends and family, fear of not leaving a legacy behind, fear of being forgotten, ... It also prompts you to take action.

You have one year to live after all, so what better time to act than now? Your emotions can leave you feeling side tracked, but they can also fuel your dreams and propel your aspirations forward. The goal is not to suppress those emotions or make them disappear, but it's rather mastering them so you can leverage their power.

So, ultimately, you can learn when to listen to the impulses and urges your emotions are promoting and when to ignore them and listen to the voice of your intellect instead. So how do you deal with your emotions when they're inhibiting your growth and obstructing your path to success? A great lesson to be learned about managing emotions comes from stoic philosophy. In fact, stoics view emotions as part of a two-stage process: the involuntary experience, and the conscious rationalisation.

The Involuntary Experience

You're about to give a presentation to a large group of people, the moment you find yourself standing in front of your audience, a flush of nerves and anxiety hits you like a wave, followed by cold sweats, a flood of thoughts, and heightened alertness. You can feel yourself choking over your words as an irrepressible sense of doom takes over you.

This is an involuntary response, just like the adrenaline surge you get from watching your favourite sports team win, just like the pangs of guilt you feel after you do something wrong, and just like the fear you experience when confronted with a challenging situation. These signals represent your body's way of letting you know you could potentially be at risk, be it mental, physical, or social. Ancient Stoic philosophers saw these emotional responses indifferently. They called them 'propatheiai', meaning preliminary passions.

Stoics described them as neither good nor bad but simply a natural way that your body uses to respond to threats and danger. These emotions are part of the human experience, they're in our nature and they should be accepted as such. The truth is, you have little to no control over your emotional response. The limbic system takes over to ensure survival. This is the same system that assisted your ancestors throughout thousands of years while they faced all kinds of challenges, so be open and willing to accept it for what it is.

The Conscious Rationalisation

The second stage of this process consists of an examination. This is your chance to analyse your initial response and decide on how you want to proceed. You have the ability to accept your involuntary experience, explore the reasons behind its occurrence, and act upon it or do something about it.

- **Acceptance**

When you experience a strong emotional response like anger, sorrow, or fear, the first step is to accept that you are currently feeling that way. Recognize that you are feeling these emotions for a reason and acknowledge them as your body's way of letting you know there is something in your life that needs to be addressed. Trying to push those emotions down will only amplify their magnitude and make you feel out of control. Don't bury those negative feelings fifty feet under and expect your mind to move on as if nothing has happened. Let them materialize in whichever way they do and accept their presence as part of something deeper and larger than a whim or a capricious manifestation.

- **Examination**

The second step in this part of the process is to closely examine the negative emotion so you can identify where it comes from and what caused it. Think about what you're feeling and pinpoint the triggers that contributed to you feeling the way you do. Is it because you're expecting others to behave a certain way rather than accepting their behaviour as it is? Ponder over your expectations and decide whether they're unrealistic or reasonable. Are you offended when another person disrespects you and refuses to listen to your ideas?

Think about why their opinion matters so much to you and examine why you want to secure validation and approval from that person. Whatever the cause is, getting to the root of what is inciting your negative emotional responses can be incredibly insightful. Sometimes, a sequence of events unfolds that triggers certain emotions you believed to have just come out of the blue. The emotional response is unsolicited, unjustified, and there's no logical explanation for it. This happens when you're in what could be defined as a normal setting, except your reactions to your surroundings are far from normal, so you feel taken by a sudden urge to cry, scream, laugh, or do something that is uncalled for.

This happens when things that, although spark a negative response on your part, affect you way too much for far too long. But, the truth is, you're not hung up on that thing itself, but rather the internalized messages surrounding it, and what it means to you based on your unique personal history and background. So, in this way, examining and analysing your emotions gives you a valuable opportunity to understand and further scrutinize your psyche.

- **Action**

The third step in the process is targeted deliberate action. You've acknowledged your current emotional state and you understand where those emotions come from, now is the time to take control and prepare a plan of action. This is essential. People often look to blame external circumstances or individuals for their current situations. They make excuses to justify their lack of action and they even glamorize the idea of being in opposition with the universe.

There is self-centeredness that comes from a vapid sense of narcissism and there is self-centeredness that comes from an intense sense of self-loathing whereas the person is convinced of how unlucky they are, how nothing ever goes in their favour, and how every outside variable is programmed to eliminate promising opportunities and only send threats, misfortunes, and dire afflictions their way.

When you're stuck in that emotional state, forever perceiving yourself as a victim, not only is your ability to view the world as it truly is distorted by your blinding martyrdom, but you're also incapable of finding the good and seeing the positives. Admittedly, many people fall into hardships because of events that are entirely outside their control, but the wise know that blame-shifting and poorly contrived excuses are of no use. They do nothing to improve the situation neither in the short term nor the long term.

How to Change Your State

Yes, you might feel some relief or even satisfaction when your negative feelings are validated, especially by people other than yourself, but that alleviation and comfort are only temporary. Constantly victimizing yourself and finding new entities to blame will prevent you from taking responsibility for your current condition. Not being able to keep yourself accountable possibilities all possibilities for progress because instead of focusing on the actions that will help you improve and change, you're hung up on why you are where you are.

As much as you'd like to be in control and have full mastery of yourself, emotions and impulses included, your natural responses will not be as heroic or as glamorous as you'd like them to be. You're going to be jealous, you're going to be scared, angry, sad, or even too excited and you may feel like a coward as a result of that fear or silly for worrying too much when there was no apparent reason to worry. It might sound arbitrary and even exhausting to constantly examine your thoughts and feelings, especially the mild emotions that don't require much scrutiny, but it matters in the grand scheme of things because the more practice you have, the better you will be at identifying the negative emotions that stall your success, those that prevent you from achieving your goals and following through with the steps in your action plan.

This isn't an invitation to question every whim and inclination you have, that will only lead to overthinking and by extension the dissolution of spontaneity. This, however, is an invitation to make a habit of exploring the depths of your mental state in terms of your self-beliefs. You can do this to prevent unnecessary emotional distress but also to prompt yourself to take action even when inaction happens to be the most enticing option. You have one year to live, would you really want to waste it listening to the whispers of your mind telling you can't do it, that people will think less of you, or that the world has it in for you?

When you listen, you relinquish some of your power to those voices, until eventually there is nothing else to yield and then you surrender. Your one-year-to-live prognosis, although hypothetical, came as a shock. It moved something in you. It made you consider the life you're living now in comparison to the life you truly want to be living. It's a scary statement, a disturbing one, it's also necessary. A declaration that makes you quiver with fear until you decide to find courage in it.

Courage is not the absence of fear. It's the ability to persist in your efforts and act in accordance with what you believe in, in spite of that fear. It's a relentless determination that incites you to push yourself past your self-limiting beliefs, past the obstacles, the anxieties, the distress, and the uneasiness. This is how you change your state, not by suppressing your emotions, not by sheer luck, not by expecting miracles from the universe, and certainly not by sitting around and doing the same thing every day while expecting to get different results. You change your state first by examining your emotions vis-à-vis your self-limiting beliefs and second by developing the courage and the ability to act productively and constructively in the face of adversity.

Chapter Eight:

How to Change Your Focus

"Most people have no idea of the giant capacity we can immediately command when we focus all of our resources on mastering a single area of our lives."

-Tony Robbins

While we all tend to warp reality in one way or another, whether it be with our perspectives, our beliefs, or our opinions, the subconscious production of these stories can influence the way we view ourselves, other people, and the world around us. Sometimes, this is simply the result of our unconscious values and experiences, but other times, it's more conscious and deliberate because we aim to distort what is factual as an act of avoidance of hard realities we'd rather not acknowledge.

The stories we create are the very reason behind our suffering. When we sculpt our own construct of what the nature of the world is, we're also setting expectations of that world, and when those expectations go unmet, they lead to resistance, anguish, and torment. Some of our personal beliefs stem from personal experiences we've had, often overgeneralizations of how life is supposed to be lived.

Marcus Aurelius once said, "The soul becomes dyed with the colour of its thoughts." Our minds dictate how our days unfold, they shape our entire human experience, much like the lens of a camera determines the quality of its pictures. A defective lens will produce poor images, and a mind saturated with limiting beliefs and negative voices will produce a life of discomfort and inadequacy.

The beliefs you hold will ultimately shape the very essence of your focus. The mental dust not only tarnishes the veracity of your judgments but also clouds your focus. Your one-year-to-live predicament might have led to the realization that life is indeed short. It puts a statement that is often overused in a new light. You're almost able to sense the evanescence of life, and in a quick second, you feel it fleeting. You don't want this opportunity to be reborn to slip right through your fingers, you try to balance everything you've ever believed in against this new knowledge.

You want clarity but you're too overwhelmed, you want success but you're dragged down by the realities of your life, you want fulfilment and happiness but the cynic in you dismisses all effort as futile. You've been chasing one thing when you've always wanted another.

You can get away from what you despise but where do you turn to? Your days are unfocused, you're not where you want to be, you reminisce on your accomplishments and as good as they are on paper, they don't amount to much in your heart, they pale in front of your dreams, and shy away from your aspirations. Having one year to live, though stressful, is a catalyst to be better. The reality many people fail to acknowledge is how difficult it is to balance our personal lives with our professional responsibilities. It's easy to overlook these imbalances and throw self-analysis aside and so we don't stop to realize that we're standing in our own way.

But being the best version of yourself and leading the best life you can imagine for yourself requires self-examination. When you're committed to re-evaluating your path, this will allow you to gain a different focus, a better one. To do that, start by asking yourself these five questions.

1. Is my time well-spent?

Ask yourself every day, am I spending my time and energy wisely? Be completely honest in your answer. If it's a no, then you need to redirect your efforts towards what matters to you. If something that takes a lot of your time and energy -unless it's necessary, isn't moving you closer to your goals, replace it with another thing that will.

The first step is to examine your to-do list on a daily basis. Identify which items are of the highest priority and which ones belong to the bottom of that list. You will probably have to take a step back and re-evaluate your responsibilities several times a week and that is perfectly fine. Use those opportunities to eliminate unnecessary distractions from your schedule.

When you have one year to live, you can't afford to get side tracked. If you want to execute your plan flawlessly, you have to be willing to let go of what does not matter in the long run. Making compromises is an essential part of the process, it also allows you to gain perspective and improve your focus so it's centred around what serves you rather than what doesn't.

2. Do I have a routine to guide me?

While you don't have to plan every second of every day, having a routine brings structure into your life and keeps you accountable so there is very little room for error. You can't control everything and you shouldn't hold yourself to that standard because it will only bring about feelings of disappointment and frustration. With that said, you're much more equipped to handle the chaos in between your mornings and evenings when you have a solid routine as a reference.

Admittedly, being spontaneous is a great quality to have, it can lead you to unexpected yet brilliantly fulfilling experiences. But sometimes, it pays to be more thorough and predictable. It's very easy to lose focus when you don't know what the day has in store for you, so a little planning can go a long way.

With that said, remember to put yourself first so you don't lose yourself in a mile-long list of chores, tasks, duties, and responsibilities. You want to ideally start and end your day with something aimed at your benefit only, be it working out, reading, meditating, or simply sitting with a cup of tea and indulging in a bit of contemplative relaxation.

Whatever form of self-care you gravitate towards, take the time to include it in your day. Finding what works for you might be a process of trial and error but it can yield tremendous benefits especially when it comes to replenishing your energy and revitalizing your focus.

3. Am I able to embrace the bad just as well as the good?

You can expect your one-year-to-live journey to be thrilling and exciting, prepare to achieve soaring levels of success, find your purpose, regain your joie de vivre, and create a legacy you would be proud of. Thinking about the positive aspect of your journey can inspire you to work harder, it can be a source of sustainable encouragement and motivation.

But blind optimism shouldn't be your goal. "What if it doesn't?" your mind asks, "Ah, but what if it does?" you want to reply, and that's a great headspace to be in. However, you also want to be prepared to embrace the bad -the doubts, anxieties, and uncertainties the fear and defeatism, the things that are far beyond your control that can jeopardize your success.

These are all factors that you need to take into account. Dream big but stay grounded. You can't leave anything to chance, even the most unlikely worst-case scenarios.

Consider all the details, always go with the old adage 'everything that could go wrong will go wrong,' anticipate and draft your action plan. Instead of fighting stress and anxiety, seek to acknowledge them for what they are, and use them to propel you forward. There is immense potential for growth in discomfort and even some amount of anxiety can help you stay sharp and focused. Flip negative situations into positive ones and find opportunities that you might have previously overlooked. Embrace the bad just as well as the good because without the first you can't possibly distinguish nor appreciate the second.

4. Am I prepared to tackle the challenges ahead?

The road that will take you from where you currently are and to where you want to be is not paved with gold. The transition may be difficult at times, which is why you need to be prepared for the unexpected. Your confidence can act as an inner compass and guide you through the challenges and hardships you encounter. It can keep you calm, focused, and level-headed.

Maintaining a positive attitude will allow you to successfully handle adversity all while keeping your cool. If you're not prepared to find the silver lining in each and every situation you're confronted with, then you will feel compelled to run for the hills at the first sign of trouble. Granted, staying positive is easier said than done, so don't just say it, but make a habit of doing it. Remind yourself and call yourself out when need be. You've always wanted to be the person that is able to see the good in everything.

So be that person and embody that state of existence with your mind and body. Focus on abundance, growth, and learning. Cultivate your observation skills, look into the optimism and pessimism of others, and dig into the qualities and virtues the people around you possess that you would like to develop yourself, but also scrutinize the flaws and the negative characteristics because they will show you what you don't want to be.

Accept the permanence of the peaks as well as the valleys, recognize their impenetrability, and understand that they're everlasting. Do not waste your energy on what cannot be altered. Knowing how to pick your battles and pick wisely, your personal approach to tackling challenges and the roads that get you to efficient solutions defining moments in your one- year- to- live journey.

5. Do I need to check myself?

Your ego can throw your focus off and put you in a position where you would rather be right than accept the truth. We've delved into how your ego can ruin your life and stand in the way of your personal development. Giving it up is an important part of the journey, and it is just as vital when it comes to recalibrating the way you think about yourself and others.

You shouldn't even want to be right all the time because progress often happens through failure. If you're not making mistakes then you aren't learning and if you aren't learning then you're stagnant, heading nowhere. Fall in love with the beginner's mindset because, unlike the expert's mindset, it yields a plethora of possibilities. There's always something new to discover, learn, and explore. These occasions can arise at times when you least expect them to and if you aren't open-minded then you're bound to miss amazing opportunities that could potentially improve your life in ways beyond your imagination.

When you're up against a wall or you're suddenly confronted with the unexpected, you need a way to change your focus. Asking yourself the right questions is part of the solution but if you want to experience a true inner revolution you need to do a lot more than that. The four steps explained below will set you on the right path to change your focus and get better results.

Step #1: Move from unconscious to conscious living

You're in a store, walking around, perusing the aisles, and then you're told to focus on all the yellow items. You have three minutes to memorize as many yellow products as possible. You sprint frantically trying to take as much yellow imagery in as possible. You have a sequence in your head, whether it be by category, by function, or alphabetically. You repeat the items' names inside your head for a while. Now you have to close your eyes, you're anticipating recounting all the yellow items, but instead, you're asked to list all the green ones. Your frustration is entirely understandable, now you have to shift your focus and review the mental picture you've somewhat registered inside your head, except you have to look at it differently.

You will most likely recall fewer green items than yellow. Why? Because you were only looking for yellow. You open your eyes and suddenly it's as if you're looking at the same store with a new set of eyes. Your focus is completely altered and what was once difficult to discern has become so apparent, so obvious.

When you shift your attention, you find yourself with a different level of awareness of and appreciation for what has always been there. Similarly, when your focus is narrow, you're not able to view the bigger picture with its potential, opportunities, joy, and fulfilment. When your focus is stuck on the negatives, that's what you'll find in your surroundings, so you'll constantly be seeing problems instead of solutions.

Your focus becomes your reality and the more fixated you are on what you desperately want to avoid the more likely you are to create that very outcome and make it a reality. Sometimes, we tend to get lost in our fears of the bad that we end up missing out on the good. Just like when you were preoccupied with finding the yellow things in the store you didn't even notice what else was there beside it. If you want to change your focus, you need to shift from unconscious to conscious living. Choose to find the good because it is there!

Step #2: Look inward instead of outward

People, for the most part, have the tendency to solve problems by trying to remedy some aspect or other of the situation. They seek to fix a certain variable expecting it to subsequently affect the rest in a similar manner. Because they look outside themselves to transform a situation that causes them trouble, their short-sighted solutions rarely work because of the limits of their control.

People will do whatever it is they do, reality will be a reality because it cannot be something else, and the only way to deflate the areas that bring us the most unhappiness in our lives is often the most neglected; that is looking inward and examining our own reactions. This goes hand in hand with the involuntary experience and the conscious rationalisation in the last chapter.

If you want to change your focus you have to have the courage to take an honest look at yourself and try to understand how you make yourself unhappy by the way you react to external stressors.

Relying on the outside world for your happiness and fulfilment is an unfavourable pursuit and the moment you decide to take back control and appoint yourself as the protagonist in your personal story is the moment you will learn to improve your focus and find happiness from within.

Step #3: Live in the present, not the past or the future

Take an honest look at the thoughts you have about the past and the future. What do you notice? They're all deeply anchored in fear and lack. The truth is your worry, overthink, analyse, judge, and doubt yourself obsessively because of those thoughts. You're convinced that what you need is not at your disposal and that any situation other than your own would be a blessing to experience. Then you run these ideas in your mind on a loop.

The chatter refuses to stop and so you're exhausted the moment you wake up, the moment you go to bed, and every second in between. Have you ever noticed the pervasive sense of quietude and peace that comes with a tamed mind? Or perhaps you've always thought it a luxury that only the ignorant are allowed.

How blissful must it be not to worry for every waking moment! You don't need an empty mind to experience joy and happiness, what you need is the ability to be in the present, and that experience is always available to you for the taking.

When you're rooted in the present moment, it feels like coming home to a place you never actually left, a place you get to know for the first time. This realization is usually overshadowed by your active thinking mind and its maddening buzzing. It forbids you from all forms of silence and even when you're alone and expect peace of mind, your furious thoughts multiply like wild mushrooms -my mind is guilty of this and it has been one of my biggest struggles. Though I am proud to say that I have worked tirelessly on silencing those nagging little voices for my own sake. But when you refrain from feeding those thoughts and allowing them to consume your attention, you're able to see the reality that was always there, clear, reliable, and undisturbed. Letting go of the past and moving away from the future to the present will create the ideal premise to renew your focus and regenerate your energy.

Step #4: Cultivate appreciation and gratitude

Becoming aware of your experience and developing your ability to examine your emotions will highlight the chagrin that accompanies your critical self. When you start to pay attention to your thoughts, you will find that not everything your mind produces is an ally. Your inner monologue can often act more so as an enemy than a friend. It will critique your every move, scrutinize your every thought, and mock your every feeling. But no matter how vicious and malevolent it gets, do not allow those voices to control you.

As you delve deeper into your thoughts, you will find negativity, shame, and disconnection. Don't let them overpower your true self. Instead, move away from criticism and judgment and embrace appreciation and gratitude. Be more open to what is happening around you, more welcoming of the present, and be mindful of the empty mental space that all that negativity used to occupy.

When you begin to live in alignment with your values, you start to notice the unlimited opportunities to express kindness. Your grudges have no other choice but to subside, the inner violence toward yourself will follow, gradually dissipating from your mind, allowing room for a clearer focus and a renewed sense of determination. You will finally feel at ease with yourself as well as the world around you.

So, how do you change your focus? It necessitates an inner revolution, one that requires as much commitment as it does openness. Openness to fail, to learn, to discover, to explore, and to grow. Looking inward is the first step, becoming aware of the patterns your mind plays out that disrupt your mental and physical well-being.

Living in the present is the second step, being conscious of the vibrant world around you with its electrifying possibilities. Letting go of the inner voice that is hurting you and causing you anguish and torment is the third step, allowing your heart to sing, being appreciative of everyone and everything, and expressing your gratitude to the universe as well as its people. Changing your focus purposefully and mindfully begins with changing those stories you've been telling yourself.

Recreate the narrative so that you're at the centre of your one-year to live journey. Make its elements serve you and your goals. Rewrite your own history, don't let other people do it for you! When you start to change your focus and concentrate on the good in life, you will find good even in the worst circumstances. You will also be a lot better equipped to solve problems and overcome hurdles that obstruct your way. So, when things get tough and nothing seems to be going your way, what will you focus on?

"Always remember, your focus determines your reality."

— George Lucas

Chapter Nine:

Discipline

"Discipline is doing what you hate to do, but nonetheless doing it like you love it"

– Mike Tyson

The premise of setting goals and making plans necessitates some degree of discipline and self-control. But establishing milestones with the concept that you have one year to live in mind is entirely different from making new year's resolutions. We tend to make the latter in a whimsical state. We like to dream about what we want to embody, how we would like our lives to be, and what our days will consist of. We think we're the ones setting those goals, but we aren't, or at the very least, we aren't setting them for ourselves. We're setting those goals for a distant version of ourselves, an ideal us, the person we want to be, not who we are. And because there is this disconnect between those two individuals, we never feel responsible for actually working towards accomplishing those goals. They're not ours and we're not tied to them.

Visualization can be a powerful tool when our efforts are focused and targeted, not volatile, and effervescent. You were presented with the opportunity to truly consider what you want in life. You were asked to write your goals down in excruciating detail. The process might have been painstaking but it also allowed you to gauge your priorities. Finding your genuine purpose and vocation is no brainstorming exercise. You can't just "give it some thought" and come to a decision that will shape the entire course of your existence. You have to be absolutely certain of where you want to end up, your destination has to be definite, precise, and clear-cut. When you know what you want, you also know that you want that thing ardently, there is an implied intense longing that keeps you in check in the long run. That's what helps you stay on track, a source of incessant inspiration if you will.

The truth is, motivation is fleeting. It's ephemeral, and you simply cannot rely on motivation alone to get you closer to accomplishing your goals. We all have good days and bad days, but it's what you do on the bad days that counts the most. This is where self-discipline comes in. It's the anchor that ensures your safety when the waters of life are murky and chaotic. It keeps you from drifting and breaking loose.

But discipline requires mastery of the self, it asks you to conquer your inner caprices and desires, particularly those that aim to entice and distract. You will inevitably want to give up, no matter how determined you are, difficulties will materialize and pressures will mount. The voices inside your head will hum, enticing whispers of self-sabotage, and like a siren's call, it will allure you to give in to those irresistible echoes.

Standing your ground will seem almost impossible, but as Plato stated "the first and best victory is to conquer self." When you manage to rise above your impulses, that will be your first triumph, one of many throughout your one-year-to-live journey. Cultivating and nurturing self-control and discipline means your resources won't be drained on futile debates like whether to indulge in activities and behaviours that aren't in alignment with your core values or goals. Discipline makes you more decisive, so ultimately you don't allow impulses and whims to dictate your choices.

You become the architect of your own beliefs and the actions you take to achieve your desired outcome. You also won't fall prey to empty distractions and frivolous temptations that only lead to temporary relief. You will feel more fulfilled and more satisfied with the direction your life is headed to.

"You have power over your mind—not outside events. Realize this, and you will find strength."

- Marcus Aurelius

Self-discipline is a superpower that once you learn how to develop will serve you for a lifetime. But where do you get this superpower? What secret force of the universe or ancient god is going to bequeath this superpower to you? As much as we like to overcomplicate matters, a certain penchant for the dramatic I must say, a proclivity that each one of us has been guilty of, acquiring self-discipline does not require you to scour

Discipline

the earth for a sacred scripture with indecipherable text, save that for another adventure.

Self-discipline comes from within, it's as simple as that. Now let's say you want to set a new goal, you have this idea that's been preoccupying your mind and you want to execute it. You feel that sudden burst of energy and inspiration, you're brimming with enthusiasm, and you're convinced this goal will be 'the one,' once you accomplish it, your life will change for the better, and success will pour over everything you do. You think to yourself, now that I am determined and motivated, I might as well reach for the inconceivable. You're riding that high and pushing the boundaries of 'no risk, no reward.' But then comes the part where you actually have to put in the effort. Your daily to-do list is impossibly long. You think you can get everything done but you're already spreading yourself too thin, so you are only able to complete forty percent of that list. Now forty per cent is great for a start, yet you don't feel as accomplished as you dreamed to be. If you only set forty percent of those tasks for yourself to do in the first place, you would have completed them in their entirety (it's basic math). But since you established unreasonable standards for yourself, you ended up feeling disappointed.

Instead of a victory, you have a failure on your hands, and the little bit of enthusiasm left to salvage won't sustain your efforts to keep working on that goal, so you declare it a lost cause and give up altogether. Once you realize that you're only causing yourself pain either by ignoring your problems or trying to be disciplined but doing it half-assedly, you will feel a calling to stop hurting yourself. That's your sign- enough of making your life worse, now is the time to try and make it better (or at least less bad for a start). Tell yourself that you are going to:

- Get to know your strengths and weaknesses
- Remove temptations as much and as often as possible
- Start taking small actions instead of big leaps
- Gradually push yourself outside your comfort zone
- Let go of destructive thought patterns and habits
- Practice daily diligence

Knowing your strengths and weaknesses

We all have our weaknesses, whether it be unhealthy food, bad habits, social media obsession, etc. It's important that you understand that weaknesses don't just consist of the areas where you lack self-control the most. These are incorporated within yourself so much so that you begin to view them as quirks or character traits, but these weaknesses have the power to hold you back and prevent you from following through with your goals.

Knowing your weaknesses can help you stop them from interfering with your ambitions and sabotaging your progress while knowing your strengths can help you capitalize on your strongest suits and leverage their potential to drive yourself forward. Self-awareness is an indispensable tool to have, though it requires constant focus and the ability to acknowledge your shortcomings. Don't pretend that your vulnerabilities are not real but don't succumb to them either.

Get to know your strengths and more importantly, own up to your weaknesses because you can't conquer them until you do!

Removing temptations

This may seem obvious but it's a necessary part of the process. By simply eliminating the biggest sources of temptation from your surroundings, your self-discipline will significantly improve. Once you've set a goal, you need to make the needed adjustments so that all the aspects of your life are working together to reach that desired outcome. If you want to get in shape and be healthier, then throw junk food in the trash and implement a solid exercise regimen. If you want to be more productive, then eliminate distractions. If you want to read more, then put 30 minutes to an hour aside just for reading every day and put your phone away. Learn to prioritize and then execute starting with high-priority tasks and low-priority low priority ones. The fewer the temptations, the more focused and consistent you will be.

Taking small actions

When you think about tackling huge and intimidating projects, you're instantly filled with a sense of dread and overwhelmed. Discipline doesn't mean you have to collect large wins every single day. Discipline is rooted in consistency and resilience more so than how impressive your short-term victories are. One of the most important steps you can take to develop better discipline is to take small actions. Like in all great endeavours, patience is key, and you have to start small and then build your way up from there. If you want to declutter your space but are overwhelmed by the daunting mess, find three areas to declutter for a start. If you want to try your hand at drawing but are discouraged by your beginner status, focus on one particular object and do it over and over again until you've perfected your technique. You will get better at cultivating your self-discipline if you focus on breaking big projects into smaller and more manageable tasks.

Pushing yourself outside your comfort zone

One of the main reasons behind our poor sense of discipline is that we have the tendency to run from difficult and uncomfortable things. Our avoidance of hardships pushes us to always opt for the easy, comfortable, and familiar. So, instead of facing our fears, we procrastinate, we push and stretch as far as we can until we can't afford to anymore. We take refuge in silly, idle, and pointless distractions that bring nothing of substance to our lives. What we fail to realize is that this escapism is ruining our lives. Though eventually, we will have to stop running and begin to expand beyond our comfort zones. There is an invaluable opportunity for growth in discomfort. And one small step at a time, you are going to start pushing into discomfort, see how it feels, understand that it's not the end of the world, and the results will be well worth it.

Letting go of destructive thought patterns and habits

Your self-limiting beliefs and destructive habits will creep in, they will urge you to quit your pursuit when things get tough. Your inner voice will tell you to put things off for the moment being. Those impulses don't serve you. Instead, work on cultivating mindfulness around the hurtful and damaging thought patterns that prevent you from unlocking your potential. See that you don't have to bend to those urges because you're in control and they are not. To develop more self-control, start by setting a time for yourself when you're not allowed to do anything but a given activity. And so, for the next fifteen or twenty minutes, you can do nothing else but exercise, meditate, practice music, etc. When you feel the urge to procrastinate or resort to a distraction, you will easily notice that urge because the rule is to do that specific task or do nothing else. You're giving yourself an ultimatum of some sort, and your mind knows it has no other choice but to work on that task so the impulses to procrastinate will begin to dissipate.

Practicing daily diligence

Discipline isn't an innate trait that we're born with, it's a learned pattern of behaviour. And much like learning a new skill, discipline requires daily practice and consistency. You have to make a habit of being disciplined, though the time, effort, and focus it takes to build that self-discipline can be exhausting. It might even feel like a chore and maintaining your willpower to stay on track will become difficult. The more challenging it is to tackle tasks that require a lot of self-control, the more appealing distractions and temptations begin to look. So, you need to work on becoming more disciplined by practicing daily diligence in the various areas associated with your goals. This goes back to taking small steps every day that will incite you to push the limits of your comfort zone and keep you accountable for accomplishing your goals.

Finding victories to celebrate in success as well as failure

One of the main reasons why people fail at developing and maintaining a strong sense of discipline is because of how discouraged they get when things don't go as planned. They feel bad about not being able to meet the standards they set for themselves and they feel guilty for not keeping the promises they made to themselves. As a result, they're convinced they're not cut out for the life they imagined for themselves and so they give up. But here's the thing, there are victories to be found and celebrated in successes as well as failures. Failing means you tried, you put in the effort, and you invested yourself in something. So, what if it didn't pan out? You can't expect yourself to succeed from the get-go. It's a process that requires a lot of trial and error. If you messed up then that means you also learned something. You're aware that the approach you took didn't work, so instead of throwing in the towel, try something different, adjust your action plan, and do it again. Let go of your perfectionism and keep going. No matter what the outcome is, see it as an opportunity to learn, grow, and get better.

Chapter Ten:

Habits

"We are what we repeatedly do."

- Aristotle

It's morning, your alarm goes off, and you reach for your phone and hit snooze. You know exactly what time it is and how far you can push it before you're running late. You've gotten used to setting your alarm ten minutes earlier, just so you can delay it a bit further. You already know that those 10 minutes won't make much of a difference in terms of the quality of your sleep. They won't make you feel more energized or more well-rested, but they've come to fill the role of what almost seems like a superstition.

Your mind needs that pattern of hitting the snooze button and the time it takes for your alarm to go off again. It's become a ritual where you mentally prepare yourself for the day ahead.

One year to live

You finally get up, reluctant and angry at your 'night self,' the one who decided that consuming four hours of trash TV right before going to bed was a brilliant idea. You wait for your coffee to brew while you're doom scrolling on social media, needless to say, your day is already off to a great start.

The coffee doesn't do much besides give you those morning jitters, and that's your cue to leave the house for a dull day at work. You're operating on autopilot at this point, there but not completely there, the only thing to look forward to is the usual cookie stop during your lunch break.

You go about your day, completing tasks and doing work that has lost all of its meaning, like repeating a word over and over again until the sound you're making becomes completely incoherent, a jumbled mess. You only feel alive when you're finally back home and your night self gets to break free from that living-dead morning zombie. You choose what to watch with meticulous detail, a sense of precision and finesse that you can never emulate when working, only when you're looking for mind-numbing content to consume. You pick your poison and lay down; the comfort and familiarity of your couch make it feel like a second skin. You're in your natural habitat at last.

You may not be aware that you even have a routine in the first place. You may view your life as chaotic and unstructured, but much of what you do is ruled by your inner autopilot. Your daily actions are governed by the habits you cultivated over time. Some are terrible, and some are less bad, but overall your day tends to unfold in the same way it always has.

In spite of the unexpected popping up every now and then, your brain seeks to bend all those external events so they are somewhat fit in with what the 'usual' looks like for you. To put it in simpler terms, your habits are those actions you've grown to do repeatedly, but also the chain of thoughts, and the sequence of decisions you take without giving them much consideration. The majority of the things you do every day comes from habits.

Habits allow you to save energy because your mind does not need to expend its resources to decide what to do, when, where, and how to do it. Often, these habits emerge and establish themselves without your consent. First comes the cue, that's what triggers a certain pattern of behaviour. That cue is what dictates to your brain the routine that is about to unfold. Next comes the series of actions that follow that cue. Finally comes the reward, which in turn works to reinforce the habits by telling your brain they're worth it.

These elements work together in a loop and that loop is what defines your habits. It's a basic concept of classical conditioning much like Pavlov's dog. There's the stimulus, there's the response, and then there's the reward. When a habit loop is formed, you begin to crave the reward that comes as a result of executing that habit. And so, the anticipation of that reward introduces the craving.

So naturally, if you want to create lasting change in your life, you need to direct your efforts to replace old bad habits with new and more productive ones. You can establish new habits by shifting your routine, but you need a strong sense of self-control and discipline to keep you from relapsing.

The power of anticipation

If you ask people who have the habit to meditate why they started meditating in the first place, you will get as many responses as the number of individuals you asked. Perhaps it's because they were feeling overwhelmed, or perhaps it's because they have the tendency to overthink. They needed a practice that would allow them to shut the inner chatter, they were in too much emotional distress and they felt like they exhausted all other avenues. They tried it out of curiosity, they aimed to strengthen their spiritual muscles, they were looking for a sense of connectedness they were unable to find anywhere else … etc.

Now if you ask them why they keep investing a portion of their day to meditate, you will most likely get very similar responses. They like the mental clarity meditation provides, they enjoy the sense of calm and quietude that comes with the act of meditating, and they like the feeling of serenity and harmony with their surroundings. They feel more accomplished, more at peace with themselves and the people around them, more in charge. They have come to crave that self-awareness and mindfulness that is free of judgment, and that untainted and pure experience was enough of a reward to make the practice of meditation into a habit.

Cues and rewards are important components of creating habits, but anticipation and cravings are at their essence. You can choose a cue that will prompt the desired behaviour you want to implement. For instance, putting your phone on silent mode and making a cup of tea before you begin reading. The reward could be as straightforward as getting a baked treat afterwards, watching a movie, buying yourself something, or simply the pleasure you get from reading something you like.

Think about that reward and the pleasant feelings that come with it, then allow yourself to anticipate that reward. Eventually, that anticipation and craving will make it easier to make time for reading and enjoy it too. The anticipation for the reward is what drives habits and figuring out how to spark that anticipation is what makes creating new habits easier. And often, we don't know the cravings that drive our behaviours until we start looking for them.

Forming new habits

The process of forming a habit can be divided into four simple yet fundamental steps:

- **Make it obvious**

Creating a new habit necessitates a cue because that's what first prompts your brain to initiate a certain pattern of behaviour. This preliminary step helps you predict and anticipate the subsequent reward. Our ancestors, for instance, were on the hunt for cues that indicated where basic rewards resided, this includes food, water, shelter, etc.

In modern-day society, we are on the hunt for cues that anticipate other rewards like money, authority, status, approval, fulfilment, etc. We are continuously perusing our surroundings for cues because they signal that we're in proximity to rewards. So, if you want to establish a new habit, you need to make the prompt for that habit obvious in the first place. To make it easier for yourself, you can begin by tying a new habit to an already existing one. Identify the patterns in your day and consider how you can use your current habits to create new, positive ones. For example, instead of checking social media while you're drinking your coffee, you could replace that with journaling, meditating, or reading.

- **Make it appealing**

This is the motivational force that will drive you to pursue that habit. Without some degree of appeal and anticipation, your brain will have no reason to enforce that behaviour. What you seek to achieve is often not the habit itself but the change in your mental and physical state that it promises to deliver.

So, in this regard, you're not motivated by exercising but rather by the positive chemicals it triggers and the physical transformation it contributes to. You're not motivated by turning your TV on and sitting in front of it but rather by the opportunity to be entertained. Each and every craving is intrinsically linked to your desire to change your internal as well as your external state. But it's worth mentioning that cravings vary from one person to the next.

People are not motivated by the same cues, goals, rewards, and cravings. An alcoholic will see a bar as a potent trigger that engenders a powerful wave of desire, for someone else, that bar might be just a convivial background for fun conversation, a designated hangout place. In this context, cues hold little to no meaning on their own, that is until they are interpreted. It's the observer's thoughts, feelings, and emotions that shape that cue into anticipation. And so, to form a new habit you need to make it appealing. Give your mind an incentive to instil a certain pattern of thought or behaviour, help it make a positive association between that and the trigger, and push it to anticipate the reward.

- **Make it easy**

Next is the response or more explicitly the actual habit you want to assimilate, this can either be a form of thought or a specific action. The routine you want to implement will occur when your incentive is powerful. So, while you're working on developing more discipline, you need to start small and build your way up. If a particular behaviour requires more mental or physical effort than you are willing to invest, then you automatically won't do it, or at least you won't feel inclined to.

As a beginner, setting high expectations for yourself will lead you nowhere. You might be willing to overexert yourself for the first few days, but you will soon grow tired, exhausted, and impatient, especially if the outcome is not as dramatic as you've imagined it to be. Drastic behaviour changes require a high level of self-discipline that often cannot be sustained in the long run. Starting with small steps will make the new habit much easier to adopt.

Being consistent is another major aspect of developing new habits. For a task to become automatic, you have to be willing to perform it on a daily basis. The more often you do it, the easier and more natural it becomes. In addition to that, what makes a habit "stick" in a sense is the removal of all friction or as much as you can manage. Friction is what stands in the way of developing good habits.

Researchers changed the timing of elevator doors in a scientific study to reduce elevator energy use so that people had to wait nearly thirty seconds (instead of the customary ten seconds) for the doors to close. As a result, workers opted for the stairs as they deemed it easier, or less frustrating than waiting half a minute for the elevator to work. While testing employees' patience was not the goal of this study, it nonetheless indicates how easily agitated we get when we are confronted with even the smallest friction in our surroundings. So, if you want to succeed at forming new habits, make the behaviour as easy as you can at first, and once you get accustomed to that pattern, you can then tweak it to achieve your desired results.

- **Make it rewarding**

The purpose of a reward is to satisfy your cravings but most importantly to teach yourself that the actions for which you're being rewarded are worth remembering. Granted, these rewards do come with benefits of their own, whether it be improving your health through exercise and a balanced diet, acquiring more money and higher status through being promoted.

With that said, your mind is more interested in the immediate benefits of said rewards, and that's the contentment and relief from satisfying your cravings and fulfilling that anticipation. Rewards also help your brain understand which actions satisfy your cravings and lead to pleasure. Because feelings of disappointment and fulfilment are part of your internal feedback mechanism, they allow your brain to make the distinction between the actions worth pursuing and those that aren't. As a result, rewards reinforce habits through positive feedback.

Habits

If a certain pattern of behaviour is lacklustre in any of these four steps, then you will have a hard time making it into a habit. Overlook the cue and your habit won't see the light of day. Decrease the craving and you won't feel the need to take action. Make it too difficult and you will feel the urge to give up. And if the reward is not worthwhile and compelling, you won't feel the need to perform that task or behaviour again the next day. Without those first three elements, then your behaviour will simply not occur and without all four it won't occur again.

Cheat Sheet

This section of the book summarizes the tools, actions, and exercises in all chapters from Part 1 that you should aim to use or complete to get the most out of this self-development guide. This represents the nuts and bolts of the book and is meant for individuals who would rather not read the entirety of this manuscript but still want the key takeaway action points to follow. Or for those who want a refresher on the book.

Cheat Sheet for Chapter One

Exercise: Death Meditation

It's your funeral. Everything is set. The casket, the chief mourners, the family bearers, the car, the guests, the flower arrangements... Visualize the scene as if you were there. You can see yourself in the open casket, you can hear the faint music. Take a closer look. Who are the attendees? You spot your family, friends, and loved ones, perhaps some of your neighbours, colleagues and former classmates from way back.

Now listen to the things they're saying about you. Listen to the words coming out of their mouths, the comments you wholeheartedly want them to make, and the things you want to hear them say about you. Take a deep breath and don't leave the scene. Simply lean back, keep your eyes closed, and focus on what you've heard (from your partner, kids, best friends, colleagues …). Now take a moment and write everything down.

What people said about me

_____
_____
_____
_____
_____

What I wanted people to say about me

_____
_____
_____
_____
_____

The takeaway from this exercise is that each thing you 'heard' and wrote down reflects a deeper part of who you are, what core values you hold in high regard, and what you would like your life to be about. What you heard other people say about you reflects your lifestyle. Perhaps some comments may have been disappointing or they may have filled you with regret. Maybe one of the people said "he had so much potential that he left unfulfilled", or "If only he could overcome his fears, I wonder what tremendous things he would have been able to accomplish." Fortunately, you're not dead yet, which means you still have time to overturn the verdict and start living in a way you want to be remembered. The reason why you need to do this exercise is also practical in a way that allows you to gain perspective into your inner workings and understand your life through the actions you took.

This next exercise builds upon the findings of the first one and will help you determine what you truly care about in life if you weren't inhibited by the things holding you back. This is definitely a scary one too (especially if you're not very fond of visualizing your own death, but then again, this is the whole premise of this book). But if you choose to go through with it, even if it upsets or unsettles you, you will connect with what matters to you in life. So again, take your time, find a quiet space for honest and open reflection, sit, and contemplate.

Exercise: Epitaph Writing

Part A

For this exercise, you will need to write your own epitaph. This is the inscription of your gravestone as it would be designed if you were to die today. What would your epitaph say if you left this plane of existence without fulfilling your goals, dreams, and passions? What would the text be if you didn't live with a purpose if you didn't lead a life that aligns with your core values and principles?

Be mindful of all the things you wanted to do that were left unfinished simply because you were too scared to see them through. Think of all the projects you've thought about starting that you never did because you allowed your doubts and worries to get in the way. Think of the self-limiting beliefs, the negative self-talk, the self-deprecation ... List all the reasons that kept you from unleashing your full potential. Then write it all down.

Here Lies

_____

_____

_____

_____

_____

This was difficult, wasn't it?

This exercise forced you to face some of your deepest fears, perhaps even a few catalysts of shame, guilt, and embarrassment. However, it was necessary. You can't make lasting changes if you don't look death in the face and fight your way back to life.

Part B

The second part of this exercise will be much more inspiring. I'd like you to rewrite your epitaph, only this time, you write it as if you fulfilled your dreams and aspirations. Write an epitaph you will be proud of, one that paints a positive picture of yourself, one that summarizes all the great things you've accomplished. Think of this epitaph as a direct representation of all the things that matter to you the most, the things you truly care about, and the things you wish to be renowned for.

Imagine you could live the life of your dreams. No fear, no doubt, no worries. What would you do on a typical day? What would you like to stand for? As you consider these questions, visualize your headstone. What words are inscribed there? What is written in your epitaph? Think of a series of statements that best encapsulate the essence of your dream life. What do you want to be remembered for? If you could live a life free of fear, what would you invest your time and energy in?

Here Lies

_____

_____

_____

_____

_____

This exercise isn't merely hypothetical. You are basically planning for your true epitaph, so what you will be known for and what defines your life are entirely up to you. It's all based on the actions you choose to take right this moment. This is how you determine what people say about you at your funeral, and this is how you (although metaphorically) write your own epitaph.

When you're done, compare the script from Part A with the script from Part B. Place them side by side and spot the differences. Not every goal you accomplish will be there, but the things that are most important to you, the things you've worked for, the values you held and lived by, will be. If you're not living a life that is true to your values, then you're not the person you want to be. Now is the time to make changes and now is the time to live the life you want and do the things that matter to you!

Cheat Sheet for Chapter Two

Below is a list of exercises that will teach you how you can let go of your toxic ego. Make sure to implement these before you move forward with this book, otherwise, the upcoming chapters won't make much of an impact if you're still holding onto those limiting beliefs.

1. Adopt a beginner's mindset
2. Focus on effort instead of expectations
3. Choose purpose, not passion
4. Ignore the talk and do the work
5. Kill your pride
6. Stop romanticizing the grand narrative
7. Learn to better manage yourself
8. Say no to what doesn't serve you
9. Don't chase credit and recognition
10. If you find yourself in a hole, stop digging
11. Check your entitlement at the door
12. Focus on your higher purpose

Cheat Sheet for Chapter Three

The wheel of life is a tool that can help you assess how balanced your life currently is. Although the perfect balance between all aspects cannot be achieved, sometimes, one aspect of your life can require most of your energy and time, which means other aspects can suffer from this, so you may feel as if your life is out of control. The wheel of life can help you gain some perspective and identify the areas that need some tending. To create your personal wheel of life, you need to examine your satisfaction in the following areas.

The Mental

- Contribution: Giving back to the community, charity work, contributions to society …
- Growth: Personal growth, learning, self-development, career fulfilment, personal and professional achievements.

The Physical

- Wealth: Financial stability, future growth in wealth, and income that satisfies your current needs.
- Health: Physical health, satisfaction with your level of fitness, efforts to maintain your well-being through sleep, exercise, and eating habits.

The Emotional

- Romantic relationship: Responsible, intimate, and loving relationship.

- Relationships with friends and family: Getting along with your family, having a trustworthy circle of friends, making the most of the time you spend with your friends, etc.

The Spiritual

- Relationship with the self: Self-respect, self-acceptance, self-love, healthy self-esteem.
- Connection with the spiritual: Spiritual guidance, connection with the inner and outer world, healthy relationship with your spiritual being.

1) On a scale of 1 to 10 (where 1 represents very low satisfaction and 10 represents very high satisfaction) rate your satisfaction with each aspect of the wheel of life. This doesn't mean the time and energy you spend on each area, but rather how satisfied you are with the quality of that category.

___ Contribution

___ Growth

___ Wealth

___ Health

___ Relationship with friends and family

___ Romantic relationship

___ Relationship with the self

___ Connection with the spiritual

2) Use the circle graph in the book to fill your rating for each category (0 being the centre and 10 being the extremity). Then answer the following questions.

- How balanced is your wheel?
- What area in your life are you most wanting/willing to make a difference in?
- What is the current state of this area?
- What do you feel is missing or not working out in this aspect?
- What is your ideal score for each category that you want to achieve in a year's time?
- Where are the biggest gaps in your satisfaction levels?
- What actions do you need to take to address those gaps?
- What does success look like (for you) in each respective area?

3) Now that you have completed your wheel of life, it's time to take action. For each area that you feel needs improvement, write down three key goals that will help you improve and bring more balance to your life. These could be as ambitious as starting a business or as simple as checking up on your friends more regularly -whatever you feel passionate about.

Side note: While I can't necessarily push you to do anything, my aim here is to guide you while you work on achieving the goals you've set for yourself. I can only specify, explain, and demonstrate, so it's up to you to follow through with this.

Mental

Goal 1

_____
_____

Goal 2

_____
_____

Goal 3

_____
_____

Physical

Goal 1

_____
_____

Goal 2

_____
_____

Goal 3

_____
_____

Emotional

Goal 1

_____

_____

Goal 2

_____

_____

Goal 3

_____

_____

Spiritual

Goal 1

_____

_____

Goal 2

_____

_____

Goal 3

_____

_____

Cheat Sheet for Chapter Four
Create Your One-Year-to-Live Bucket List
Step 1: Write it down

Step 2: Pick a number of goals/aspirations

Step 3: Dig deeper for ideas

Step 4: Finalize your bucket list (and prep for execution)

Practices for Mental Wellness

Exercise your mind

Invest in something you've always wanted to learn

Practices for Physical Wellness

Do a little resistance training

Replace unhealthy options with your favourite fruits and vegetables

Practices for Emotional Wellness

Stop waiting for that magic moment to save you

Find your purpose

Take action

Trust your instinct

Put yourself under scrutiny

Practices for Spiritual Wellness

Start your day with gratitude

End your day by writing down one thing you are thankful for

Cheat Sheet for Chapter Five

The Mental Actions to take

- Limit your social media exposure
- Read knowledge and books you absolutely enjoy
- Write and journal about your days

- Always stay positive, no matter what
- Steer clear from unnecessary conflict
- Always be in the moment, neither in the past nor future

The Physical Actions to take

- Walk at least forty minutes every day
- Stay active as much as you can
- Be balanced in your exercise routine
- Follow your doctor's orders but be open to alternative opinions -not all doctors know everything!
- Take care of your body with proper hygiene and maintenance
- Don't be afraid of changing your wardrobe into something you enjoy having on
- Continue working if needed in order to provide for yourself or others if needed
- Seize every moment you live

The Spiritual Actions to take

- Spend time meditating daily
- Read or listen to the works of philosophers you connect with the most
- Keep a gratitude journal
- Listen to your instincts more
- Let go of envy

The Emotional Actions to take

- Never skip family gatherings
- Spend time with your family
- Make amends
- Literally, tell the people you love how much you do
- Show the people you love how much you love them
- Value your relationship with your significant other
- Plan as many experiences with your significant other as time would allow
- Forgive others you've clashed with

The action plan for taking action

Step 1: Write each goal in your to-do list in a separate paper or section

Step 2: Under each goal, write every step you can take right now or as soon as possible

Step 3: Hold yourself accountable for everything you've set out to do

Step 4: Start with the smallest and easiest goal

Cheat Sheet for Chapter Six

The following steps will help you while reflecting on your goals and measuring your progress:

1. Practice self-awareness
2. Study the trends

3. Assess progress
4. Evaluate your technique
5. Adjust your timeline
6. Track your progress using journaling, habit-tracking apps, planners, detailed schedules, etc.

Alternative ways to assess your progress

1. Define what success means for you on a daily basis
2. Create new metrics to measure your growth and development
3. Answer these three questions on a daily basis: How am I feeling? Did I do what I wanted to and how much of it? Did today matter?

What is your Plan?

Write it Down

....
....
....
....
....
....
....
....

Pick a number of goals /aspirations

....
....
....
....
....
....
....

Dig Deeper for Ideas

....
....
....
....
....
....
....

About the Author

Growing up in the charming town of Gorleston-on-Sea, Richard's early life was filled with the comforts of home-cooked meals, cherished moments with his family and unforgettable fun with friends. His lifelong dream was to serve in the Royal Marines, with aspirations of joining the elite Special Boat Service (SBS). However, a medical setback, an underactive thyroid, abruptly closed the door on his military ambitions. This unexpected twist in his life led him down a different path, one filled with adventures and uncertainty.

In the aftermath of his military dreams being dashed, Richard embraced a phase of vibrant nightlife and social revelry, becoming a self-proclaimed party animal. While these years were marked by fun and excitement, they also brought about an element of unpredictability to his journey.

Amidst the partying and revelry, Richard explored a multitude of job opportunities, from working in restaurants,

About the Author

hotels, and pubs, to the marine industry, cable technician roles, and more. It was during this period of exploration that he discovered the corporate world.

The corporate environment served as a platform where Richard could channel his energy and passion to make an impact. Over time, he honed his skills and developed a deep commitment to personal growth and self-actualization. His remarkable journey culminated in him becoming a guiding figure in the world of training, coaching, and personal development strategies.

Currently based in Pune, India, Richard has influenced the lives of many through his mentorship. In addition to his corporate role, he's the visionary founder of two thriving enterprises. One is Impact Vertex, a global business training and coaching organisation. The other is Cobra Thai, an MMA and Fitness Gym brand with two thriving branches in India and a mission to create many more. Richard's life is a testament to the transformative power of self-discovery and seizing the opportunities that come one's way.

END

www.ingramcontent.com/pod-product-compliance
Lightning Source LLC
LaVergne TN
LVHW061611070526
838199LV00078B/7238